# Why I Went to Prison
## Living in a Chris Christie's New Jersey

by Marjorie Parise

**RoseDog❋Books**
PITTSBURGH, PENNSYLVANIA 15238

RoseDog Books
585 Alpha Drive
Suite 103
Pittsburgh, PA 15238

Visit our website at *www.rosedogbookstore.com*

ISBN: 978-1-4809-7156-1
eISBN: 978-1-4809-7133-2

# ACKNOWLEDGMENTS

There are a few people that I have to thank. Without them I could not have made it through this very trying time in my life. The first and foremost is my husband, Rob. He made the grueling trip to Danbury every weekend to visit me, sometimes twice a week on very little sleep. These visits are the only thing an inmate has to look forward to and it helped me get through each week – one at a time. Rob never wavered in his love for me or his support of me.

I want to thank my daughter, Kristina, and son, Robert. Their words of encouragement gave me strength on a daily basis. Somehow they always knew just what to email or say to me on a phone conversation that helped me dry my eyes and know that everything will be OK. Knowing what they know about the circumstances you will read about, they were never embarrassed of me or ashamed. I am very proud of them and thankful that they have grown to be the amazing young woman and man that they have become.

I need to thank those that wrote to me on a regular basis, whether it was a four page letter or just a card to say "HI". Each of you have no idea how much it meant to me and how much it helped me get through the days. I read your letters and cards over and over again. You know who you are. Thank you.

I would also like to thank Thomas Rolston. He has helped me by doing extensive research and by writing some of the text. Thanks for your time and knowledge Tom.

Finally, I thank our dear friend Barry Bender who has helped us in many ways. It is hard to find true friends and he has shown us time and time again that they do exist. Thank you for all you have done for us.

# Why I Went to Prison
# Living in a Chris Christie's New Jersey

Corruption, Extortion and Racketeering –
all used as a means of Torture in New Jersey.

**Note:** This book has an associated web page called www.whyiwenttojail.com. This site contains video and audio clips, along with documents and pictures that are referred to in the text of this book. You will see references to these files throughout the book. They will tell you where on the webpage to go to see, hear, or read the appropriate file. All documents and pictures can also be found at the end of the book. Thank You.

# INTRODUCTION

**"F**irst off, this is when we realized … this was never about money," – Robert Parise … But it was … in the end … somewhere around $50 million dollars and Governor Chris Christie allowed his friends to get their hands all over it.

Mine is the story of a loving house wife, a mother of two and the owner of a small construction company who was sent to jail for Bankruptcy Fraud. I spent two years in Danbury Federal Prison, then a few weeks in hell's cesspool at a half-way house in Newark, New Jersey. Most people think of federal prison as a country club – but I can assure you that is not the case. In the winter there is no heat and you are given only one blanket. In the summer temperatures can reach well over 110 degrees and there is no air conditioning. Ice was a privilege which inmates were seldom afforded. Most of the food we were given to eat had expired. The posh conditions of federal prison most people hear about are reserved for celebrities - not for people like me. I was to be tortured.

This book is the story of why I went to Federal Prison. My story involves political corruption, extortion, and a major "land grab" in Ocean County, New Jersey. All of this was accomplished with the blessing from none other than New Jersey Governor Chris Christie. It shows his direct involvement while he was the Federal Attorney for the state of New Jersey, sanctioned with the "strong arm" support of the Political Boss who runs Ocean County, George Gilmore, in the execution and cover up of crimes committed by both elected and appointed public officials. My story shows how both of these men were involved directly in sending me to prison for two years. It also shows the sickening depth that political corruption existed, and continues to exist here in New Jersey, and how the current Federal Attorney turns a blind eye to all of it. In short, this book is the story of a "whistle blower" who got in the way of the "machine" and was severely punished for it.

New Jersey's Governor's rise to office was premised on a campaign promise to end corruption. As the US Attorney for New Jersey, Chris Christie prided himself on his prosecution of political corruption. Christie was clearing the road for the day that he would run the state. All of the actions he took as Federal Prosecutor to achieve this end were violations of the law. Those who set me up and made sure I went to jail never saw a day of jail time for their crimes, and every one of them was politically connected to Chris Christie in one way or another – from the local township officials all the way up to the current US Attorney, who let Christie off the hook for the Bridgegate affair. Chris Christie himself came in at the end of what can only be described as torture I was being put through and put an end to an investigation that we had started with the FBI that would have incriminated his "friends and family". Obviously, I would receive no justice.

Christie's war on corruption – politically and criminally - was just a way of weeding out the competition, so that he and his friends (Political Bosses, Freeholders, Township Officials, Federal Prosecutors, Local Law Enforcement and so on) could rape, plunder and pillage all the fruits of the Garden State. Because I stood up to their crimes, and said "NO", I went to prison. The documentation I speak of in this book was too damaging to "them" to allow me to remain free.

# CONTENTS

# 1. OPENING ARGUMENTS

At the time this book began I was serving a two-year sentence at Danbury Federal Prison. I was originally charged with Structuring and Bankruptcy Fraud. I took a plea deal on the bankruptcy charge that spared me the possibility of spending 10 or more years behind bars. I have been asked numerous times, "If you were innocent, then why did you take a plea deal?" On the advice of my attorney I was told that I would only get a short time under house arrest. I took the plea deal to end the nightmare I found myself in and to avoid the possibility of spending a decade or more behind bars.

Everyone who had a hand in sending me on my journey towards incarceration was directly connected to Chris Christie and George Gilmore. They have created a system to enrich themselves while everyone else takes the fall. Many of those responsible for sending me to prison were part of the US Attorney's office in New Jersey – where Governor Christie remains heavily rooted. "They" also have ties to both federal and state courthouses, as well as federal and state law offices. Governor Chris Christie runs those as well.

There isn't a newspaper or media outlet that hasn't reported on Christie's questionable behavior. The late Senator Frank Lautenberg once labeled Christie as "the name-calling governor," and "the king of liars." As told in The New Yorker magazine, as a child, growing up in Newark, New Jersey, Chris Christie was a bully when he didn't get his way. Once a local diner owner kicked Chris Christie and his high school friends out of the place for hanging around when they weren't spending any money. So what did Christie do? As Class President he organized a boycott of the diner. The diner had to reach a settlement with Christie and his goons or face losing business. What did this teach Christie's friends? It taught them to pay attention and he would show them all how to get anything they wanted. Then there was the time that Christie's spot on the high school baseball team was threatened by a transfer student. Christie and his father tried to block the student's enrollment. Thomas Kean, former Governor of New Jersey, once said about Christie, "He doesn't always try to persuade you with reason. He makes you feel that your life is going to be very unhappy if you don't do what he says." I can say with all honesty that the last statement is true. Having gone to prison because the Governor's friends weren't getting their way, I can say with all my heart that they made my life so … not only unhappy, but completely unbearable at times. I certainly will never forget the unnecessary hardship thrown my way at every turn.

Chris Christie's friends on local government boards blocked construction plans. His lawyer friends took my money, stonewalled my cases in court or failed to push forward allowing contracts to expire all in the interests of Christie's friends. There were his contacts at the local court houses that made sure a friend of Chris Christie was sitting on the bench. Then there were his friends that ran the banks and held mortgages on properties destined for construction. Then, of course, there were Christie's friends in law enforcement that can make up any charges they want. My daughter would have been the Incredible Hulk to have actually perpetrated one driving infraction she was accused of. All I did to deserve this attention was buy two pieces of land that "they" wanted for themselves. I found out the hard way that "they" control most of the real-estate market in Ocean County, New Jersey. Chris Christie isn't so welcomed in Northern New Jersey, but down along the Jersey Shore, his friends run just about everything. Who buys what, who pays for what, who gets their applications processed, who gets proper legal representation, who gets to make up lies about your family, "they" control. "They" control the town commissions, and the towns themselves. Any lawyers "they" did not directly control would drop clients as to not end up on "their" shit list.

People like me who are smart – or perhaps dumb - enough to collect evidence that clearly incriminates Christie's friends become persona non grata. Mark Weber of The Progressive said it best: "…that the man craves these conflicts – especially with women." Whatever it is that "they" have against women, they make no bones about hiding it. I'm a woman and when "they" discovered it was me and not my husband who owned a very successful construction company – the methods of torture were piled on. The torture leading up to my incarceration was all because I stumbled upon a massive land grab in Ocean County, New Jersey. I thought I was being extorted by one local politician, but as time went on, I realized how high up the food chain this case actually traveled.

Christie's ill treatment of women has been well documented. Even early on in his political career, as Christie was running for Freeholder, he produced a TV ad that accused Cecilia Laureys, an opponent in the Freeholder race, of being investigated by the Morris County Prosecutor. There was no such investigation. Laureys lost the race because of the lies contained within the ad. She would later go on to sue him for defamation. As part of the settlement, all Christie had to do was publicly apologize in local newspapers. I tried suing all of his friends and the settlement I received were three hots and a cot. I even had recordings from my private investigator of Christie's friends bragging and laughing about how they were torturing me.

Assemblyman Anthony Bucco once described Christie's way of doing things as "character assassination." I was a female business owner. I am a mother of two and a loving housewife. In a short period of time I was made out to be a criminal, charged with Structuring and Bankruptcy Fraud. After the charges were filed - and made as public as possible - everyone who ever knew me no longer saw me the same again. It felt like fifteen minutes after the charges were filed, every local newspaper was running the story. It was almost as if the news outlets knew the verdict before I did.

Character assassination is an understatement. My daughter now has drug charges on her record for a crumb of marijuana that couldn't get a mouse high and my son was charged not once but twice with bringing weapons to two different high schools. My son didn't even attend one of the schools he was accused of menacing.

Again all of this is nothing new. Christie showed the world his ability to create lies about people and his obvious disdain for successful women not long after entering office. In 2010, Christie publicly badgered a young female teacher who approached him asking questions about his policy on education. The demeaning response this poor woman received from the newly elected Governor, shaking his finger in her face, was nothing more than wave after wave of lies.

Christie once spoke publicly that someone should "take the bat out" on 79-year-old State Senator Loretta Weinberg. Then there was the time a local woman named Gail, who simply asked Christie about why if he sends his own kids to private schools is it fair that he should cut funding to public schools. Christie's response was "It's none of your business." He then made the rest of his tirade about himself and his beliefs. Let's not answer the question about school funding. Let's just make sure we make this woman feel as shitty as possible and embarrass her so every one of her friends and neighbors can see that this is what you get when you go up against the Governor.

Of course, who could forget the time that Christie's character assassination targeted the medical opinion of Doctor Connie Mariano, calling the former White House Physician a "hack" who was only out for her fifteen minutes of fame. Here is a woman who was hired by the highest office in the land to provide medical opinions to the President of the United States and Christie brushes her off, insulting her entire career. All the while Christie's goon squad can been seen behind him in the video nodding their heads in approval. One man behind Christie on the dais was a police officer. You don't need a college degree to be a police officer. But you need several college degrees to become the White House Physician. All Doctor Mariano said was that because of Christie's weight problem he could die at any moment. But when that police officer was nodding his head in agreement, I was outraged. Heaven forbid that police officer's life is on the line; he'd be lucky to get an opinion from Dr. Mariano, a Naval Officer and a Commander and the Division Head of Internal Medicine and Director of the Internal Medicine Clinic at the San Diego Naval Hospital. And here "they" were, for all the world to see smiling, nodding their head in agreement to all the lies Christie was spewing. She was the Personal Physician to three American Presidents and three American First Ladies.

Another example is Ed Tamm, Jr. He ran against Christie for Freeholder in the Republican primary. Christie ran a campaign ad stating that Tamm and his fellow board members were under investigation. Once again, this was a lie. Christie was sued for deformation of character and lost.

To further my point I have one name – Jamila Davis. She was a real estate broker/straw buyer that at times helped people with low or bad credit buy a home. Davis is yet another woman that the Christie administration made a public example of. She is currently serving a twelve and a half year sentence for mortgage fraud. Christie himself said of the verdict, "This is a long prison sentence that appropriately matches the breadth and complexity of the fraud committed." No one who has ever known Jamila Davis would say that she is a criminal genius. So, if her sentence matches the crime, then why was it that all of the MEN, a real estate agent, a mortgage broker and a corrupt real estate attorney, were never charged or indicted in her case? It was these MEN that helped her create all of the false documentation that allowed her to commit fraud against Lehman Brothers Bank – a bank that collapsed because of shoddy business dealings. Davis herself feared that the documentation she was coached into creating was "shoddy" at best and more than likely would be rejected. Nope, her mortgage broker pushed the paperwork through without a second glance. Without their mentoring and connections, she would have never known how to beat the system.

The connection between Ms. Davis and I was that she was coached into creating all the documentation that sent her away. I too was coached by crooked lawyers, forensic accountants, and various members of state and federal law enforcement in how I should proceed. I too would later find out that all of these parties had ties to Christie. And again, like Davis, all of the people who gave me the advice that sent me to prison were MEN. None of them ever did time, nor were they ever indicted for the extortion and racketeering scheme unleashed upon me, and others like me.

And even though I never knowingly committed a single crime, I was forced into a position where I had to admit guilt. My bankruptcy attorney knew there was never any fraud. And this is when the prosecutors began to over-charge the penalty for the crime. To get you to agree to admit to some form of guilt, "they" come at you so hard that they make your life unbearable. I was willing to say or admit to anything just to make all of the "torture" go away. Prosecutors threatened me with years and years behind bars if I didn't admit to some wrong doing. "They" had all the evidence and all the witnesses they needed to make good on their threats. Like Davis, all of the people who were claiming to help me were the ones taking the witness stand against me now.

Knowing this now, I shouldn't have been surprised when soon after I bought a piece of property in Waretown, someone called me on the phone threatening to make my building process damn near impossible unless I consented to their demands. Here was one of Christie's friends, the Waretown Land Use Board Chairman, calling me up and threatening me that they would stop me from using my property. Later, when someone from the Asbury Park Press newspaper contacted Mr. Summerville to ask about the phone conversation, he denied making it. When they shared with him that they had phone records showing that he did in fact make the call, he said that he called to congratulate me on doing such a wonderful job building another house up the street from his. Funny thing was, his own building department in Waretown, NJ was failing me over and over again on the inspections of the home I was building. If what Mr. Summerville said to the Asbury Park Press was true, then why were they failing me and holding up the building process? Actually, as a member of the Land Use Board, he was violating the law in making any contact of this type. Mr. Summerville should have been brought up on charges for making the call. He should have been another "notch" on Christie's list of accomplishments in his prosecution of political corruption. Yet, Summerville remained free and I went to prison. That call was a blatant conflict of interest, as he sat on the board that was in charge of approving or disapproving my applications. This is all part of the process in which they torture people. Summerville had already denied my application the night before he made the call.

Torture was the word "they" liked to use every time I hit one of the "bumps" they threw in the road. I owned a small construction company specializing in custom homes. Corrupt Government Officials like Mr. Summerville could throw so much red tape in your way making it impossible to navigate your business. There are some basic rules in the business I chose to be in. The most obvious was, in order to build homes you need to buy land. In buying two pieces of property in Ocean County, New Jersey it led me to residing in one of the smallest custom homes I've ever stayed in – a jail cell. You see, there were "connected" people who lived near the land that I bought. Those people envisioned something different than I did in how the land was going to be developed. Hence the topic of conversation with Mr. Summerville. Also, Mr. Summerville and his friends thought that if they applied a little pressure perhaps they could make a bit of extra cash by charging additional fees to help you cut the "red tape". The extra money I was charged was used for improving the infrastructure of the street – a street where most of the Waretown Land Use Board members and Mr. Summerville lived. To make things worse, I later found that these repairs / improvements were completed at a fraction of the cost that they extorted from me and the rest of the money disappeared, not to be accounted for to this day.

Here's how the "game" worked in a nutshell: You own a piece of property and guys like Summerville fine you, they rezone your property, they make it impossible for you to develop it or sell it to anyone. Then they have a third party come in and grab it from you for pennies on the dollar. For example, there was an older couple who lived across the street from the property in Waretown. If they were to have sub divided their property it would have been worth about $2.5 million dollars. This couple wanted to retire and cash out. However, Waretown Mayor Dan Van Pelt would have none of that – he wanted this piece of land as well. Mrs. Wojciechowski confided in me that Van Pelt was doing the same thing to them that he was doing to me. The torture had become so bad that Mr. Wojciechowski had to be hospitalized. In order to prevent any more torture, the Wojciechowski's sold their property to US Homes (currently the Lennar Corporation) for far less than it was actually worth. At the closing of the property, the Wojciechowski's signed the paperwork and before the ink was dry, Van Pelt walked out of a back room and the property was signed over to the township instantly. Sound like collusion to you? More to follow on the Wohciechowski's.

Van Pelt and his cohorts were in the business of systematically obtaining smaller parcels of land like puzzle pieces, then packaging them as a single parcel that they would "flip" to well-known large national developers for big dollars. We later found out that Van Pelt had been trying to sell the Wojciechowski's land before he owned it or had even approached them to have a contract drawn up on it. In my case, it reached the point where I could do nothing with my property, so I decided to cut my losses and sell the lots in Waretown "as is". Shortly thereafter, word got back to me that potential buyers were being turned away by "them". To find out how deep this went I hired a private investigator to act as a potential buyer. He was "wired" and he recorded all of his dealings on tape. On one such tape, I have Waretown Mayor, Dan Van Pelt, bragging about how "they" were torturing me over the properties. Again, because of evidence like these tapes, it was imperative that I be "put away" and put away I was.

When you become one of the many who have been incarcerated, you lose not only your freedom; but, your family is now saddled with the moniker of having someone behind bars. I played by the rules. I followed every law. I hired lawyers who were supposed to work in my best interest and, because of the corrupt political climate in Ocean County, I was sold "down the river" and lost everything I worked for in my life including my freedom.

Many members of my family shunned me over the case. I have five brothers and sisters who have walked away from me, not to mention friends who I've had for over twenty years who did the same. My kids are indifferent about the family. And those who put me behind bars knew this – so it is one more thing that they took from me. You reach the point where you are not even thinking about the money you were robbed of; you are worrying about how you and your family will survive once you get out of prison. But, "they" left no stone unturned in inflicting the maximum amount of pain and anguish on me. In the blink of an eye, "they" made sure both my dental x-ray license and my driver's license were suspended, making it close to impossible for me to return to the workforce once I was released. I initially got my x-ray license because these "friends" of Chris Christie forced me out of the construction business and I needed a way to support my family. So, I went back to school to obtain my dental assistant certification and my dental radiology license.

I have voice recordings on tape of their wrongdoings. Those speaking on the recordings talk with pride about what they can do to hurt someone. On the tapes they openly admit to wrong doings with complete strangers. I have all the paperwork that proves I did everything legally. It really is sad that even with evidence that a blind person can see is a clear case of extortion and railroading, I still ended up in prison. In order to railroad someone you need to master the art of collusion and racketeering. "They" have done this to others so frequently that it's become a proven "game plan" that they use over and over because it is presently "fool proof".

As defined on WIKIPEDIA:

> Collusion is an agreement between two or more parties, sometimes illegal and therefore secretive, to limit open competition by deceiving, misleading, or defrauding others of their legal rights, or to obtain an objective forbidden by law typically by defrauding or gaining an unfair market advantage. It is an agreement among firms or individuals to divide a market, set prices, limit production or limit opportunities.[1] It can involve "wage fixing, kickbacks, or misrepresenting the independence of the relationship between the colluding parties".[2] *In legal terms, all acts effected by collusion are considered void.*

As defined on WIKIPEDIA:

> A racket is a service that is *fraudulently* offered to solve a problem, such as for a problem that does not actually exist, that will not be put into effect, or that would not otherwise exist if the racket did not exist. Conducting a racket is racketeering.[1] Particularly, the potential problem may be caused by the same party that offers to solve it, although that fact may be concealed, with the specific intent to engender continual patronage for this party. An archetype is the *protection racket*, wherein a person or group indicates that they could protect a store from potential damage, damage that the same person or group would otherwise inflict, while the correlation of threat and protection may be more or less deniably veiled, distinguishing it from the more direct act of *extortion*.

Racketeering is often associated with *organized crime*, and the term was coined by the *Employers' Association of Chicago* in June 1927 in a statement about the influence of organized crime in the *Teamsters* union.[2]

I provide these definitions as a reminder to those who know and for those who want to know. The last definition we need to keep in mind is BULLY. We all know what that means and it means something different to us all. In this case you take the example of a kid who grew up in the difficult neighborhoods of Newark, NJ. According to biography.com, Christie was given a quote by his mother that was meant for finding true love and he turned it into an idea that would define his leadership style. A style that would suit perfectly for what is Ocean County, New Jersey politics.

As quoted by Christie himself "she told me that love without respect was always fleeting, but that respect could grow into real and lasting love ... But I have learned over time that it applies just as much to leadership. In fact, I think that advice applies to America more than ever today." How does Governor Christie get respect so that true love "could" one day grow? Squash everyone who gets in the way and imprison those who can offer any proof that there was ever something going on in the first place. From the moment Chris Christie was elected to low level office he started perfecting his ability to reduce his opponents to rubble.

Let us not forget what went on in Hoboken, NJ. Because at the heart of the Hoboken case lies the methods and the lessons for sending a mother of two to jail: A redevelopment study conducted by numerous Christie appointees found that of all the areas within the city of Hoboken damaged by Super Storm Sandy, only one parcel of land was deemed worthy for development money. As it turned out that single parcel of land was owned by the Rockefeller Group. The Rockefeller Group has given large amounts of money to Christie for various campaign purposes.

The property that I bought in Waretown was manipulated the same way as Hoboken, and then miraculously ordinances regarding how the properties could be subdivided changed. Mr. Summerville tried to get me to buy a piece of land that was later sold to 8th District Assemblyman and Mayor of Waretown, Daniel Van Pelt, using the very same game plan.

Chris Christie has built an incredible wall of respect around himself. At least he thinks of it as respect. It's really more like fear. Those that find themselves within those walls are protected. But, you can be expelled at any time and, because you may know some secrets, you have to be discredited immediately. No matter if you've been a long-time friend or someone he just met, if you cross "them" your character has to be destroyed so that they can look as though they stopped corruption at any level. Daniel Van Pelt can tell you that. He was the main "extortionist" that we had to deal with. Van Pelt was extorting tens of millions of dollars in property from local citizens. Because our investigator caught him on tape in their conversations, he became a "cancer" to Christie and his cronies in Ocean County. He had to be "surgically removed" from the picture so that not too much pain would be inflicted on him and so that he would not "spill the beans" on the entire operation in Ocean County. You've heard the expression, "loose lips sink ships." That's why when he was indicted his house sold in cash for twice what it was worth in a time when housing prices were collapsing by the second, and why Van Pelt's wife, who at the time was a sitting Ocean County Judge, was able to keep her cushy job serving Ocean County even though she participated in conversations with her husband and Solomon Dwek, a "setup" man brought in by Chris Christie. These conversations eluded to bribes for facilitating illegal wetland permits. Dwek was a wired FBI informant who posed as a developer attempting to create a list of local politicians willing to take bribes for services and easing of restrictions in the development of land parcels. It is more than likely that conversations like the ones between Van Pelt and Dwek is what leads elected and appointed Government Officials in Ocean County to believe they have impunity in building homes on wetlands. Dan Van Pelt was the Mayor of Waretown at the time when James Mackie, then Director of the Ocean Township (Waretown) Municipal Utilities Authority, built his home on Bay Parkway. Mackie's house sits on nearly three acres of highly sensitive wetlands in an estuary where there are no other houses.

**see: www.whyiwenttojail.com CHAPTER 1 - PICTURES 1-2**

Let's talk about how people's reputations are ruined. Bridget Anne Kelly was a very high ranking official in the Christie Administration. She was once his Deputy Chief of Staff, but she was recently quoted as saying, "I will no longer allow the lies that have been said about me to go unchallenged." This young lady was indicted for conspiracy, fraud and other charges in relation to the closing of the George Washington Bridge back in 2013. Her statement speaks about the lies that were obviously made up about her to assassinate her character. Christie threw her under the bus to cover his own wrong doing. With me they went a step further as you will learn later in the book.

There are two lies that I'll always remember most. The first was when the Lacey Township Police contacted my son and told him they wanted to talk to him about possible child abuse charges against his girlfriend's parents. When he went to the Police Station in Lacey, the officer started reading Robert his rights. When we questioned why this was happening, we were told that the police department had received an anonymous letter from Trenton stating that my son had been overheard discussing plans with another girl who attended Lacey High School to murder his girlfriend's parents. This conversation was supposedly overheard in Lacey Township High School. My son never attended Lacey Township High School. He attended high school at Ocean County Vocational Technical School (OCVTS) which is located on the Lakehurst Naval Base. Obviously the letter was not true. This made no difference to the police in Lacey, as they had a plea agreement already written up before we got there. It was written even before he had a chance to appear before a judge. He was forced to sign a Probation Before Judgment form that we were told would clear his record in six months.

The second lie came one year later. Someone actually called OCVTS, the high school my son was attending on the naval base, claiming that he had guns in his locker and that he was going to kill students. When his locker was opened nothing was found. The Federal Police (because the second threat involved a Federal facility) investigated who had made these calls and were leveling these accusations against my son. The Feds found sophisticated equipment was being used in the making of the phone accusations, obviously so the perpetrators could avoid being traced. The Federal Police did have the ability, despite the efforts of the caller, to trace the call. This would have been impossible if the call was made almost anywhere else.

Shortly thereafter, the investigation into who made the call against my son was stopped. The person or persons responsible for making the calls, as we were told, had been identified at that point. My husband and I couldn't understand why the case would be halted. Much later on, when this story was shared with Associate U.S. Attorney for New Jersey, Joseph Gribko, who just so happens to be the person who pushed forward my indictment, all he had to say on the matter was that "it was not his office that stopped the investigation". However, it was obvious to everyone in his office when he made that statement that he was certainly aware of the incident. Getting any kind of justice for my son was never going to happen. More on Mr. Gribko later in this book.

Now we will go into how I was fleeced of all of my money. Over the years leading up to my incarceration I paid approximately $750,000 in legal fees to those who I thought would properly represent me. Apparently the oath of Attorney/Client privilege meant nothing to these lawyers. Most of them had conflicts of interest as they had positions with numerous Townships that I was litigating with. A prime example would be as follows; I was given a recommendation by New York Attorney, Joseph Bondy (whom will be referred to frequently later in the book) for a high profile defense attorney in New Jersey named, Henry Klingerman. Mr. Klingerman was given confidential information on my husband by Mr. Bondy. Klingerman was to be the second attorney to Mr. Bondy on a potential civil rights case – so information had to be shared between the two attorneys. Mr. Klingerman was on the case less than 24 hours when he shared some of this confidential information with a third law firm (friends of his) that were prosecuting me at that time. My husband and Mr. Bondy had arguments over the sharing of this information. Bondy argued that Klingerman would never violate the trusts between an attorney and his client until we produced a recording of my conversation with Mr. Klingerman where he admitted he shared the information because "no one told him not to".

**see: www.whyiwenttojail.com CHAPTER 1 - AUDIO 1**

The lawyers I met with during my ordeal at one point or another suddenly would claim that they no longer handled cases like mine. I was like a dead fish in the water and here "they" came, the sharks, to take another bite (meaning money) before nothing was left. I would pay one lawyer his fees for service only to have him drop me as a client, but not before he recommended me to another lawyer, only to pay those fees and get dropped as a client once again. Later I found out that all of these lawyers were friends and had numerous business dealings with the very same people who were trying to take my land that I legally purchased. So when I wanted to believe that this was not about money, boy was I wrong. "They" all got paid for services not rendered.

Just when I thought "they" had finished with their character assassination; just when I thought that all the means of torture had been used up, the following happened. In 2008, my husband and I were involved in a major car accident. We were the only car stopped at a traffic light and a woman hit us in the rear going 50 mph. The impact pushed us 30 feet forward into the intersection, totaling our car. Luckily no one was coming across the intersection. Otherwise, my husband and I would have been killed instantly. Perhaps that was something "they" really were after.

In a normal world (other than Ocean County, New Jersey), she would have been at fault for such an infraction. When the accident report was filed, the Stafford police officer claimed that the accident was our fault. Also, the woman who rammed into us was supposed to be from the town of Farmingdale, NJ. Now imagine getting hit from behind and being told you are at fault. Imagine losing a mint condition 1969 Corvette because someone hits you from behind and it's your fault. All of my friends who read the report said the same thing. "The cop must've known the woman who hit you." My answer to them was, "how could that be, she lives in Farmingdale?"

Months later at a deposition regarding the accident we found out that the woman actually lived in Waretown, NJ. It immediately threw up a red flag.

Again, this all started with my purchase of land in Waretown. Here "they" were again, inflicting more torture. It was our fault for being stopped at a red light. I was hit from behind and blindsided by one thing after another during my ordeal. I had followed the laws to the letter in purchasing property in Ocean County and I ended up going to Federal prison. The men responsible for creating one of the biggest economic meltdowns the country has seen since the great depression – not one of them went to jail – and they were the ones cooking the books on a grander scale. They got bailed out using your and my money. Me, a wife and mother of two, who buys a piece of land to build some houses on – no I'm actually the better choice to be put behind bars.

The Waretown property was only one piece of land "they" were interested in. They were also interested in an additional piece of property I had acquired in Little Egg Harbor, NJ. So, having it be our fault for sitting at a traffic light and being rammed from behind causing serious injury, was just one more thing they could do to us to bleed us dry before taking both pieces of land. The tactics used for gaining control of the Waretown property were the same ones used in Little Egg Harbor. Mirror images of each other.

# 2. THE PROPERTIES –
# WHERE IT ALL STARTED

In 1998 I started a small construction company specializing in sub-contracting and building custom homes. Starting this business was a dream of mine. I had worked as an Administrative Assistant to the President of a development company located in New York City by the name of Kellogg Properties, Inc. I had been working for the president of Kellogg for approximately 24 years and, because of what I learned and my experience there, I became familiar with all of the aspects of the building process – or so I thought. I should say that I became familiar with all the legal aspects of the building process. The politicos of Ocean County New Jersey would give me a fine education on all of the illegal methods of the building process in the years to come after my service at Kellogg.

After I started my company, when the money was good it was really good. My family and I thrived. And when the market went through its ebbs and flows, you did what you had to, to keep business flowing – but it was never terrible. In 2002, a real-estate agent that I had been dealing with for some time had approached my company with a piece of land located in Waretown, NJ. The offer was for four acres of prime land only a few short miles from Long Beach Island (LBI), NJ, one of best vacation/beach spots on the Jersey Shore. For the price and what I could make sub-dividing the land and putting custom homes on each one of the lots, I'd have to be a fool to pass that up as a business owner. Plus at this time the housing market was in good shape. There was some money to be made. But there was a catch as we found out later. The land just so happened to be on the same street as many of that Township's Land Use Board members.

It was around this time that another friend, Julius Robinson, an Attorney friend of mine had come into possession of 28 acres of land in Little Egg Harbor, NJ. Julius foreclosed on the property from another client that had started a subdivision on it. Mr. Robinson asked me if I would like to have it. Again, another sweet piece of land at a great price. There was money to be made; but, "they" weren't going to let it get away.

Who better than to handle legal red tape than a lawyer? My company hired Attorney Thomas Gannon, whose office was in Toms River, NJ, to represent us in court and handle any red tape that may come up during the proposed subdivisions on the properties in Waretown and Little Egg Harbor. Thomas Gannon was recommended to me by Brian Rumpf, who at the time was the Mayor of Little Egg Harbor, NJ. Rumpf is currently an Assemblyman who ran on the same ticket as Daniel Van Pelt for the Assembly seats. At the start of my torture the same names kept popping up. Brian Rumpf's wife was, at the time, a Land Use Attorney representing Little Egg Harbor as well. She heaped on the praise that Gannon would be perfect for us because, "he knows everyone." To further set the stage, Gannon would later be sued by me for malpractice, but I digress.

The sale to me of the Waretown property was contingent on the present owners signing off on the subdivision application. Once the land belonged to my company we could turn it into a four-lot subdivision, where we could build four homes. For some reason, the township was putting pressure on the current owners to kill the deal and, because of this, the owners refused to sign off on the subdivision application.

Mr. Gannon went to court for us at the County Courthouse in Toms River, NJ to ask the judge to simply force the original owners to abide by the signed contract and sign the subdivision application. For a lawyer as high up the food chain as he claimed to be, this part of the deal should have been completed with a hand shake over a cup of coffee with the judge. However, the ironic part of all this is that Gannon testified during a later deposition, that even being a Land Use Board Attorney in the towns of Lacey Township and Tinton Falls he knew very little about Land Use Laws. As a result, I learned a valuable lesson the hard way: whenever your lawyer goes to court for you, be sure to be there – especially if you've only been working with that person for a short period of time. I was not in court that day, believing the legal fees I paid to Mr. Gannon were enough for him to honestly, truthfully and lawfully litigate on my company's behalf. I felt I could trust him enough so that my family and I could enjoy a much needed vacation. Who knew at the time that this would be one of the last vacations I would be able to take for a long time. Certainly Mr. Gannon knew everyone, I only wished, if his deposition statement was truthful, that he knew more about the laws he was supposed to be applying to my case.

We later found out that Mr. Gannon, on that day in a Toms River courthouse, was trying to convince the judge to allow the original motion from the Waretown property owners to stand, which would allow them not to sign the subdivision application. My husband and I would later go down to the courthouse and get the transcripts from the hearing. One of Gannon's quotes to the Judge was, "I told my client to fish or cut bait." Rather ironic for someone practicing law in Ocean County.

First of all, he was supposed to be working for us, not working for the township. Secondly, for some reason he was stalling the subdivision application. It was the exact opposite for which he was being paid part of that $750,000 I forked over to crooked lawyers on my way to prison. Without that signature the contracts would expire and the property could be sold to someone else, in particular, Daniel Van Pelt, Mayor of Waretown. How could I go from a done deal to potentially losing a very lucrative piece of property practically overnight?

My husband, Rob, and I went down to the courthouse and asked to read the transcripts from the stenographer. There it all was in black and white. Mr. Gannon, who I had paid legal fees to for his services, was now fighting for the very people he was supposed to be opposing. If not for another lawyer sitting in the courtroom listening to what was going on we would have certainly lost the Waretown property. This attorney had the courage to interrupt the proceedings on our behalf. Perhaps he saw, as we later read in the transcripts, that something just wasn't right.

This lawyer questioned Mr. Gannon's understanding of the laws in Waretown. This lawyer even questioned the judge as to why this case could not move ahead when the contract was clear. The attorney saw taxpayer money being wasted by Mr. Gannon's stonewalling. It was simple; all the judge had to do was order the original owners to sign the subdivision application as was agreed to in the contract. This anonymous lawyer questioned the judge as to why time was even being wasted on the contrary to the contract. What you have to understand is that, as the Wojciechowski's discovered in their case, all of the judges in Ocean County are appointed with the approval of the South Jersey Godfather, George Gilmore, and follow his orders.

17

After all was said and done, for some mysterious reason, the judge forced us to close on the Waretown property without the subdivision application, contrary to law, otherwise the contract would expire. Almost seems like my attorney, the judge and Van Pelt were in collusion, doesn't it? Part of the rule surrounding collusion involves the limiting of competition by deceiving, misleading and defrauding others ... to gain an unfair market advantage. If we had lost the property to Van Pelt, he would have been able to acquire it at bargain basement prices.

Right after the purchase was finalized we discovered that the Waretown property had been rezoned into one acre parcels. This was an attempt to limit how much development could be done on the parcels. The land had previously been zoned as one-quarter acre; but, the funny thing was that we only planned to build on one acre parcels to be cost effective. Later they tried to force two acre zoning, but we were already approved under the one acre zone. Again all of this was set up so that construction would be delayed and I could be defrauded and extorted out of my property.

Once I became legal owner of the property – the nightmare began. I could not get permits on any of my properties throughout Ocean County. All of the inspections on new construction were being failed. On one project, I was being failed for steel constructed buildings, when all of the houses were constructed of wood. There was failure after failure. "They" did everything to hold up my homes, and in turn shut down my business. That's when I decided to bail out and just sell the land. We had many potential buyers, but our real estate agent was being told that the Township was bad mouthing me and the property, basically steering people away from the sale.

Knowing this, I decided to hire a private investigator by the name of Ross Bowen to uncover whether or not these accusations were true. Ross was a retired law enforcement officer who started his own private investigating company, Bowen Investigations. Bowen took on the case although he was a bit apprehensive at first. He sent an investigator in as a potential buyer. You will read more detail on this later in the book.

When we finally got before the Waretown Board for our subdivision application, for some unknown reason, Attorney Gannon did not show up. Because of his absence, the Board refused to hear our application. The Board went on to cite deed restrictions that had been already released by the property owner who put them there in the first place. Lies were being invented about the deed restrictions so the Board could refuse to hear our application. After the refusal, the Board opened the floor for public comment so that residents could speak about the subdivision. This is odd in itself – because if the Board refused to hear an application, then why would you open the floor to comment on it? A neighbor to the property in question stood up and started speaking. He requested that the township should hit us with maximum assessments on the property and that he was against the subdivision. The board instructed him to state his name, as they didn't know who he was and that to speak publicly he had to share his name and address.

This gentleman was Stafford Township Detective, Gordon Von Schmidt. He was the only one to speak at the hearing against my subdivision. Von Schmidt went on about how we should be assessed at the highest level because I was looking to make profits in the town. What we found out later is that Gordon Von Schmidt was a Land Use Board member at the time. Collusion anyone? The Board sat there and pretended that they did not know who Gordon Von Schmidt was. He was planted in the audience. How could the Board not recognize one of their own members? Better yet, Mayor Dan Van Pelt was sitting in the back of the room with a huge smile on his face. He didn't recognize his friend and neighbor, Von Schmidt, either? Gordon should have been instructed to sit down and not speak due to conflict. However, the Board went along with the fraud. They needed someone to give them a reason to hit us with higher assessments and further defraud me out of my hard-earned money. Gordon Von Schmidt was later recorded by my private investigator. He said that at this board meeting he told my husband that "he was greedy and hard to work with". He said that he further stated at the meeting that I should only build two houses on the property. Von Schmidt stated "what was the difference if I only made $100K or $200K dollars less." Sure what was it to him, it wasn't his money. The audio tapes of the meeting clearly show that my husband wasn't even at this meeting he was referring to. On the tapes Von Schmidt also stated that the Waretown property was long and ugly, "Who would want it?"

Later in a lawsuit against Mayor Van Pelt and another cohort, during a sworn deposition, Defense Attorney Guy Ryan stated that he was given minutes of the same Land Use Board meeting by the Township Attorney, who was then Greg McGuckin, a very close friend of Chris Christie. The minutes Ryan were given by McGuckin stated that Von Schmidt was told to sit down and he was not allowed to speak as he was a board member, but he was told that his wife could get up and speak. The Official Township recordings of this meeting prove that none of this ever took place. This wasn't the first time nor would it be the last time that meeting minutes were falsified to achieve their goals. Von Schmidt's wife wasn't even at the meeting. Guess who now owns a piece of the Waretown property, acquired at an enormous discount? Gordon Von Schmidt, of course. I guess those ugly properties had some redeeming value after all. This is racketeering at its purest form. Here was a man, a police officer, who swore an oath to protect, serve, and uphold the law, and he was blatantly violating the law by ripping me off. He wanted the property cheap and he got his way.

**see: www.whyiwenttojail.com CHAPTER 2 - AUDIO 1, DOCUMENTS 1-1a**

My company, in around 2003, hired another law firm named Fox and Rothschild located in Atlantic City, NJ. Fox and Rothschild finally got the subdivision approved on the four acre piece of land in Waretown, NJ. However, as a condition to the approved subdivision I had to pay an assessment of nearly $23,000 for my portion of paving the road in front of the property. The property was located on a gravel road. Fox and Rothschild told me that this was an illegal assessment, but that it would be too costly to fight it. I was told by my attorney to just pay it and get the subdivision finalized. So essentially, my lawyer instructed me to pay a bribe. The local township officials had fought for years to keep the road unpaved, so why did they now change their minds? We later found out that paving the entire road only cost $3,200. Who had set the price at $23,000 for me? My company paid the $23,000 and I have the cancelled check to prove it, so where did the extra money go? Again, to date, it is still unaccounted for.

**see: www.whyiwenttojail.com CHAPTER 2 - DOCUMENTS 2, 2a**

Now we thought we were free and clear and that we would get our subdivision; but, this was not meant to be. In walks James Mackie, head of the Municipal Utilities Authority in Waretown, NJ. Days before my subdivision was to become official, Mackie notified me that he was not signing off on the plot plan. In order for any subdivision to be finalized the MUA has to sign off on the plot plan. Mackie stated the reason he wouldn't sign off is because of public water lines. The final resolution for the property was approved with the installation of water wells. The law specifies that "if you are not within 200 feet of public water lines, the MUA has to sign off on the property" and allow me to build with wells that I would have to install.

Mackie discovered that my project was moving forward. He refused to sign off and claimed that he was going to run a public water line to the property. The existing public water line was approximately one-quarter of a mile away. Mackie claimed that my portion of the line, which is 480 feet, would cost about $30 thousand dollars. This is an outrageous cost for the amount of materials needed to complete 480 feet of water lines. Anyone in the construction industry will tell you that a job placing 480 feet of water lines should only cost a few thousand dollars. What Mackie did is called "splintering" the contract. Splintering is when you break up each portion of the contract. It would give Mackie a waiver on submitting the parts of the project up for bid and then he could give the work to whomever he wanted, keeping it all "under the radar". I have him recorded on a taped telephone conversation telling my husband that doing business this way will "keep everything under the radar." So much for Christie's war on political corruption. Every part of this was completely illegal. When I questioned Mackie as to how crazy the price was, he said I could get it done cheaper, but then I'd have all that "red tape" to deal with. He was actually threatening me. Mackie stated the first piece of red tape would be having my engineer draw up a proper plan that I would then have to submit to the Township Engineer. He knew time was tight on this project. He would certainly make sure that the Township Engineer took his sweet time going over my "proper plan." Then of course I would have to go to board meetings, and I've already stated how those turned out for me. There was no time for all of this and it all costs money, money I really didn't have to spend. So, Mackie said that if I pay the $30 thousand, he could bypass the "red tape" and he would sign off on all permits and get me approved. I have my husband on tape asking Mackie that, "if I pay you the $30 thousand you can cut the red tape?". Mackie's answer, "correct." Mackie can be heard telling my husband that he had the ability to get all of this work done without using an engineer. How is that safe or even legal? The fact is, Mackie was trying to hide the real cost of the project and trying to make a nice profit for himself.

Later we found out that the complete water line project for the entire block on which my property sat only cost the town $10,000. I paid the Municipal Utilities Authority $27,000. The entire job should have cost one third of what I was being extorted for. So, based on the size of the property that I owned, my portion of this $10,000 payment should have only been $2,000 or less. Just as I said earlier, a few thousand dollars. I was forced to over pay so that "they" would cut some red tape. My money went to giving Gordon Von Schmidt,

Mayor Daniel Van Pelt, Summerville and other Waretown Land Use Board members that live on that block free public water lines to their houses on my dime. Later I was told by some people that I knew who worked on the job, that Von Schmidt and his neighbors installed two water lines to each of their houses. One line was hooked up to the water meter and the other line bypassed it and was hooked up directly to the house. That way when the water company checked the meter, these guys only got charged for the trickle that went through the metered line. My husband went out to the site and saw the lines for himself. Every drop of water used in the home was free of charge. Actually, it was on me!

**see: www.whyiwenttojail.com CHAPTER 2 - DOCUMENTS 3-3a, AUDIO 2**

Later, Mackie resurfaces again, on another piece of property, where water and sewer lines are existing right in front. Naturally, after our previous encounter, I push back and when I do Mackie makes a statement that I still can't believe to this day. I have him on a taped phone conversation saying that we do not understand the "ultimate power" he possesses in Waretown. The arrogance is frightening.

**see: www.whyiwenttojail.com CHAPTER 2 - AUDIO 2a**

Twenty seven thousand dollars is what I finally paid to the Waretown Municipal Utilities Authority to have this work done for them (again, I have the cancelled check). All of this money should have been placed into a township escrow account. I never received a statement on this escrow account. All of the money just disappeared. I understood later how my money could just disappear. Gregory McGuckin, Chris Christie's buddy and the Waretown Municipal Lawyer, told a friend of mine at a Waretown Council meeting that my money was "a gift to the town" and he didn't have to account for it. Now, why would I give a gift to people who were threatening and extorting me? McGuckin would go on later to retract that statement. His story changed and he said that my money was won in a lawsuit. There was never any lawsuit filed by me against Waretown. The only lawsuit I filed was against Dan Van Pelt and another cohort personally. I mentioned the deposition for this lawsuit earlier. Gregory McGuckin covered up that the money was stolen from me and he would not account for its current disposition or what it was used for.

Here is Chris Christie's best friend ripping me off. Waretown is run by Chris Christie's friends, who believe they can violate the law at will because of the protection afforded them by their "big buddy". The arrogance they show is sickening. "They" got my land and I got two years in Federal Prison thanks to their "big buddy".

Because of the zoning changes intended to stop my project, Daniel Van Pelt was now presented with a problem. He owned the property next to mine – the same piece of property that Mr. Summerville wanted me to buy and beautify. His problem lied in that, his buddies rezoned the Waretown piece into one acre lots. Van Pelt's lot was only three-quarters of an acre. Legally speaking, Van Pelt should not have been allowed to build on that parcel of land. However, that didn't stop him from building. First thing Van Pelt did was state that there was an over-lap in the property lines between his property and mine. He wanted me, in essence, to surrender part of my land to him. Gregory McGuckin would probably call this type of activity "a gift". What Van Pelt did next, through his friends in the Toms River Court House and in the Ocean County Clerk's Office, was move the property lines over so that he had his one acre lot. And since the people in the County Clerk's Office don't notify you, I didn't find out until much later in the process that Van Pelt had stolen my land. The only thing I'm grateful for in all of this is that Van Pelt did time in jail... but none of it was for the crimes perpetrated against me.

After I decided to sell the four acres in Waretown, there were so many people vying for this piece of property I thought selling it would be a breeze. That's when the next "enigma" arose. I discovered that people who were interested in buying my property were being told to stay away. As previously mentioned I have Gordon Von Schmidt on tape telling my PI, who is acting as a buyer, that the land isn't worth anything because it's ugly. The local Township Committee and Van Pelt himself were also making up lies to potential buyers. At one point we went to the DCA (Department of Community Affairs), who should have investigated this. They actually did and the investigator even informed us that they would be filing charges against the township for their behavior. But wouldn't you know it, Van Pelt had a no-show position on the DCA and put a stop to the investigation. The investigator was shipped out of the area. He was taken completely off the case. This would happen to me again and again on my journey towards incarceration.

At this point I began recording every conversation that came to my home phone. My private investigator was wired every time he went out to pose as a buyer. I recorded everything I could from my cell phone. This would eventually become the foremost reason why "they" needed me to go to prison. What my investigator recorded almost certainly was what led to my time behind bars.

Then there was the property in Little Egg Harbor to deal with:

For almost one year attorney Tom Gannon did nothing to push our subdivision application through in Little Egg Harbor. It was troubling enough to have our lawyer stonewalling the Waretown application but on top of it he was refusing to do anything on the other subdivision application in Little Egg Harbor. My faith in Mr. Gannon had already been used up but he was still listed as my counsel and I still paid for his services. Mr. Gannon sat back and watched while the town of Little Egg Harbor was rezoning the 28 acre property.

Because Mr. Gannon failed to protect my rights, Little Egg Harbor was given free reign and rezoned my land out of its usefulness, meaning we would not be able to build homes on the land at all. So, as in Waretown, I looked in to this ruling as well. I called the Township Engineer, Tom Maroldo, to help shed some light on why my application was being held up. He told me that Joseph Coronato was the Township Attorney and that he was in charge of the subdivision application and that I needed to speak with him. I also called Scotty Esposito, the Little Egg Harbor Township Code Enforcement officer and Head of the Building Department. Scotty told me that the property had been previously sub divided and approved for its previous owner, just as Julius Robinson, the man who led us to the land in the first place, had told us. There was also a cul-de-sac and a road already cut into the land. Scotty told us Joseph Coronato was the man to speak to. In his words, "he is the man who is handling this." I found it strange that during this phone call about the land Scotty put me on hold and when he returned to the phone, he informed me that he can no longer find any information about any previous subdivision. He suddenly also had no knowledge about my information. All he could repeat was that Joseph Coronato was the man to speak to. I could tell by the way he spoke over the phone that he was told to keep quiet and was washing his hands of me.

**see: www.whyiwenttojail.com CHAPTER 2 - AUDIO 3**

After my conversation with Scotty Esposito, I knew Mr. Gannon certainly wasn't going to represent my interests. My property had been zoned "one and three" zoning. This means that some of the property was zoned for one acre and the rest of the property was zoned for three acres. But, the town had an ordinance that when a piece of property is spilt zoned the owner or the developers can use the zoning which is more beneficial to them. In my case I would have picked the one acre zoning. I could have built more houses and made more money. I paid the township almost $8,000 in application fees. This money also disappeared with no trace. After the submittal of my application, the Township had 45 days by law to deem the application complete or incomplete. If after 45 days, the township did not move on the application, by law it should be deemed complete and I would have my subdivision. Gannon never made a move on this either. What I found out, because of the split zoning ordinance, the township was using this to their benefit. When projects done by people connected to Christie and the Ocean County "machine" needed to get approved, they used this ordinance. However, the very same people, with the Township's help, challenge this ordinance to block others from getting anything done. This ordinance comes in and out like a yo-yo for these guys. They pull it out when they need it and then they put it away until someone gets in their way, like me.

Research I did uncovered several faxes between Joseph Coronato, Howard Butensky and the Township Engineer. Joseph Coronato is currently the Ocean County Prosecutor. He was, at the time this was going on, the Township Attorney for Little Egg Harbor. Howard Butensky was and remains an Attorney in Little Egg Harbor. The faxes focused on my subdivision application that was being held up in the courts. The documents I found clearly stated that both of these gentlemen knew the property subdivision application existed and was being held up for no apparent reason. But, how did they know about our case? Howard Butensky was an attorney who represented several interested buyers for other properties we owned, all of which the contracts fell through. He also represented sellers of properties we were interested in purchasing and those deals were killed by Butensky also. At one point we uncovered a fax to the Township Engineer from Butensky asking the engineer, "What the engineer was doing for Joe Coronato on our 28 acre subdivision?" Why was Butensky interested? He had nothing to do with this project.

**see: www.whyiwenttojail.com CHAPTER 2 – DOCUMENT 4**

Here is some background about Howard Butensky. He sat (and continues to sit) on the board of directors for Shore Community Bank. Shore Community Bank plays a role in my incarceration as well. I have been told that Little Egg Harbor Township is basically run by two people, Joseph Mezzina who was the

Chairman of the Little Egg Harbor Township Municipal Utilities Authority (MUA) and Howard Butensky. Even though they have no official titles in the town, everyone will tell you that nothing gets done in Little Egg Harbor without their approval. Much earlier something suspicious happened that I wasn't really wise to at the time. It was connected to the very first piece of property that I went to purchase in Little Egg Harbor. We were buying a piece of land on Nugentown Road for $55,000. Our attorney on this matter was Ron Bernardo whose office is in Lacey Township. We were a few days away from closing when I got a strange phone call from Bernardo stating that he could no longer be my attorney and that the land owners were no longer interested in selling me the land. Bernardo gave no reason and said that if we wanted to fight this we would have to get another attorney. I decided not to fight and the property was instantly sold for $60,000 to a development company called Buena Vista Homes. Buena Vista Homes is owned by Joseph Mezzina. The property was later sold to Ocean County for $400,000. Joe Mezzina made one heck of a profit - $340,000. That's why I was shoved out of this deal. I told you there was money to be made. Later on I will discuss the numerous other properties that were sold to Ocean County for huge profits using tax payers money.

Unfortunately I was naïve to what was going on. But, now Little Egg Harbor had one more trick up their sleeve for me. A friend of mine (who shall remain anonymous) called me on the phone and told me that my 28 acre property was up for tax sale. I said that was impossible as I paid all of my taxes. What "they" had the tax assessor in Little Egg Harbor, Joe Sorrentino, do was assess my property as 21 lots (as if I had received the subdivision) instead of just the one big lot that I owned. The Township made this tax assessment for that year and the previous year. This action left me with an enormous tax bill. The township knew that they do not have to notify land owners by registered mail. All the township has to say is that the notification was mailed. Yeah, like "the check is in the mail".

Since I didn't dispute the ruling, because I was never notified, the township claimed they had every right to apply this assessment. This was done even though my subdivision application had never been heard before the board to date. How could they get away with this? The "operatives" in Little Egg Harbor knew about what was happening to me in Waretown. They all knew that I was running out of money. So the only way for me to stop the tax sale was to pay this enormous tax bill and then hope to win it back by challenging it in court.

I then hired the law firm Fox & Rothschild (as in Waretown), who took this to the tax appeal courts in Toms River. This firm had some pretty heavy hitters in the legal world and this should have been a simple case. I did not have 21 lots, so how can I be taxed on 21 lots? Mysteriously Fox & Rothschild lost this battle and said that there is nothing that I can do. I hired another law firm, Schaferman Lakind, who bled me dry. Schaferman Lakind charged me $5,000 to have their expert tax attorney review the situation and inform us that there was no way to win this case. This didn't sit right with me, so I took it to court in Trenton on my own. There I found myself before a judge that wasn't bought and paid for. He asked the Township one question, "Does the woman have 21 lots or not?" The township attorney for Little Egg Harbor started giving the judge a lot of nonsense. The judge repeated his question then added, "If she doesn't have 21 lots return her money." Even with a Judge's orders, it took me two years to get my money back. Now I was aware that all of the attorneys that I was using were all owned by "them". In fact, in a deposition with Fox & Rothschild, their attorney stated that he got a phone call from Joseph Coronato saying that Thomas Gannon was a friend of his and a friend of the town. Even though they knew he committed malpractice, they wanted to get him off the hook. How deep does the collusion run?

**see: www.whyiwenttojail.com CHAPTER 2 - DOCUMENT 5**

I then called Mr. Coronato. Now mind you this man is now the Ocean County Prosecutor, appointed by Governor Chris Christie. While I was on the phone I had approximately thirty pages of documents related to my subdivision application that had Joseph Coronato's name on them as well as my own. In a taped telephone conversation with Mr. Coronato he denied ever knowing anything about my case. Coronato told me that he knew absolutely nothing about my subdivision application and that he is not the one handling it. He then hung up on me.

**see: www.whyiwenttojail.com CHAPTER 2 - AUDIO 4**

If Coronato knew Thomas Gannon, and he knew about Gannon's malpractice, then how could he not know about my case? Coronato told Fox & Rothschild that they wanted to give me some sort of subdivision. This way Gannon would not be sued and K&R Homes, me, would be happy. The big law firm, Fox &

Rothschild, held a meeting with the township engineers, my engineer, Joseph Coronato, my real estate agent and my husband who was representing me as I was unavailable. They discussed how they were going to give me a subdivision. Now you think a big law firm like Fox & Rothschild would document that type of meeting and provide some assurances. They didn't. After this, I was finally put on the schedule to be heard before the planning board. Now I was thinking I'm going to get my subdivision after all this time. But, the night before our meeting I got a phone from Fox & Rothschild's attorney saying that they forgot to send out the 200 foot notice list required by law. This is a list that you have to notify everyone who lives within 200 feet of your property that they can be at this meeting as well. This is basic lawyering 1-0-1. And they failed miserably ... or did they? I was taken off the Little Egg Harbor Planning Board calendar. They failed to protect my rights and then allowed Little Egg to hammer the property with rezoning and additional ordinances. My attorney's excuse was that the Township Tax Assessor, Joe Sorrentino, was on vacation and that a list could not be produced. Fox & Rothschild had 90 days in which to do this. They were also supposed to pay a $25 fee to get the list. They couldn't even produce a canceled check to prove they tried to get the list. This is supposed to be a huge respected law firm. All of this should have been done right from the get go.

After my conversation with Mr. Coronato, I begin having major problems with building inspectors and township engineers constantly hitting my company with fines and violations, which in turn, lead to my workers constantly redoing work over and over again on projects that were already on-going in Little Egg Harbor. Just like in Waretown (see I told you they were mirror images) the names of the players change but the plot is still the same. Coronato and company robbed me of my land and now they were going to drive me out of whatever business I had left. I was being failed on inspections. I had one buyer on a house located on Magnolia Court in Little Egg Harbor that we could never get a CO for. That buyer had to live in a hotel and eventually had to walk away from the purchase of the property. The delays the township were throwing at me forced him out of the deal. Who could blame him?

I found out that at this point, most if not all of my properties in Ocean County were spot zoned. Spot zoning is completely illegal. Spot zoning is when you take a small piece of land and you just rezone that lot, but every other lot around it is left alone. For instance, in Waretown, I had a corner piece of property on Barnegat Beach Drive. I was first told by Larry Leonard, the Head Code Enforcer of Waretown, that I had to go and get wetland permits. Now mind you Mayor Dan Van Pelt was the one selling the rights to build on wet-lands (as in Solomon Dwek). Then I found that other people were told that wetlands permits weren't needed for the same piece of property. I got the per-mits anyway. We thought we could start building, but when I submitted the building permits I found out that the property had been rezoned. This forced me to get a variance. It took me two years from that point to get the variance. And what my engineers discovered was that every other piece of land surround-ing mine was grandfathered in and not rezoned. Mine was the only one re-zoned. Thus, an example of spot zoning.

After two years of trying to get the variance and finally getting approval, my attorney, Francis Hartman (Is anyone keeping track of all the lawyers I had to go through?) never checked the resolution and missed that the Township changed the set-back number which is the distance from the house to the prop-erty line, making it different to what was applied for and approved on the vari-ance. Because of this, when I went to get building permits, I was denied. I was then told that I had to start the variance process all over again. How could such a seasoned attorney miss this? I was also told that my wet lands permits had expired, so I had to go about getting new ones of these as well. Hartman never informed me that he was an ex-Township attorney throughout Ocean County. I am really starting to think there isn't an honest lawyer in the state. So now, not only did I have to get a new variance and new wet lands permits for this piece of land, but for all of the properties I owned in Ocean County. So, after spending tens of thousands of dollars, I now had to start over again and spend even more money. And who was the Township attorney on all of these rezon-ings? Brian Rumpf, the same person who gave me Thomas Gannon, the same person who ran on the ticket with Dan Van Pelt for Assemblyman and the Mayor of Little Egg Harbor.

# 3. THE INVESITGATION BEGINS – MINE THAT IS

I had to know what was really going on. I was no longer willing to play fair. They certainly weren't. As stated earlier, I hired a private investigator, Ross Bowen. I recorded as many phone conversations as I could. My investigator pretended to be a potential buyer on the properties. It's with these recordings that "they" knew I had to be made an example of. I have Mayor Daniel Van Pelt running his mouth about how I was tortured because of these properties. I have township officials - James Mackie, head of the MUA - asking my husband for contributions to cut the red tape. I have high ranking law enforcement personnel – Gordon Von Schmidt Police Lt. Stafford Township - clearly saying that because I may have to cut down a few trees I need to have something done about me. My house was broken into several times, in what I believe was an attempt to find my tapes and make sure there isn't a juror alive who would hear them. You be the judge. The police never once investigated who broke into my home – there isn't a piece of evidence that states an investigation ever took place. I had to write a letter to the Ocean County Prosecutor in an attempt to get someone to at least look into my case. Weeks later a detective came to my home and dusted for finger prints – yup, he couldn't find a single print – not even mine. Case closed.

## The Initial Recordings

My decision to begin taping conversations and recording phone calls began when we started to hear from my real estate agent that people were interested in buying my properties. However, my agent also told me that potential buyers were being pushed away. Of course we tried to tell any and all potential buyers to cooperate with us, but they did not want to get involved. We asked anyone interested in the property what they were being told. I asked each of them if they could at least put something in writing. No one wanted to help or get involved.

The private investigator I hired, Ross Bowen, had his associate go into the Waretown Building Department and act as a buyer. It was right from the moment Greg entered the office that what we had been hearing was proven true. Greg was treated, as we can only assume, in a manner that all other potential buyers were treated. Barbara Wolfred, the Township Secretary, held her fingers up to him in the sign of a cross as if to say "devil" stay away. This woman was gesturing as if she knew that my property was cursed. Had we been able to we would have asked her more as to why she would behave so unprofessionally. As most people know it is against the law to turn potential property buyers away. It's a form of discrimination. For Barbara Wolfred to hold up her fingers in the sign of a cross and force a potential buyer away is not only crazy; but, certainly something the Township Secretary knows is against the law. Ross and Greg began digging into the backgrounds of all of the players involved.

My investigators knew who was building next to my property in Waretown. Van Pelt was building a home with a tennis court and an in ground pool on the property. Interestingly enough, town ordinances clearly state that no fence in the area shall be higher than six feet. I was being failed left and right on my property; however, Van Pelt was allowed to surround his tennis court with a ten foot high fence and not be failed. Van Pelt's home sits on only three-quarter of an acre. He was violating his own one acre zoning laws by putting in the house, not to mention the tennis court and pool. He created those laws so he certainly knew about them. Yet, he was never failed for any violation.

My investigators were good. They knew all the right things to say. They even figured out Van Pelt's daily schedule so that there was no chance of missing him. Van Pelt would always come home around five in the afternoon and, since his property butted up against mine, all Greg had to do was be seen walking the property pretending to be a buyer. Ross would sit in his car a few blocks away. Greg was wearing a wire and Ross had all the recording equipment with him.

The first conversation with Van Pelt was set up to look like a coincidence. But, when you catch someone off guard, you get the most out of them. Again, "they" weren't playing fair – neither was I. Dealing with these types of situations made me a bit nervous and we needed them to talk. So that's why my husband is heard on most of the tapes and not me. The trick to get someone to incriminate themselves is just to make them feel as though you recognize their status/importance and keep them talking. My husband had a knack for keeping them on the phone and talking. Greg posed as an over-eager buyer who was more than ready to lay down money and give them everything "they" wanted. Somehow my investigators discovered that Police Lt. Gordon Von Schmidt, who lived next to my Waretown property, liked horses. So that was the story that Greg set up – he was a potential buyer that wanted to purchase all or part of the property and raise horses on it.

At the very start, Mayor Van Pelt saw Greg walking the property. Van Pelt walked up to him, introduced himself and then instantly went about bashing my husband and his reputation as a builder. I own the company, but to all of the people mentioned from here on out, my husband was the face and voice of the company.

My investigators had to do some name dropping in order to get to the big fish. But, they weren't the only ones name dropping. Van Pelt's eagerness to open his mouth and sound like a big shot dumped other officials into the pot. Van Pelt told my investigators that, "The Deputy Mayor [Robert Kraft] is looking at a piece of this land. He likes one of these two lots." Now Van Pelt has incriminated the Deputy Mayor. On tape Van Pelt can also be heard saying, "I don't want him building," and "If I had the money I would buy the property just to stop him from building." As it turns out Van Pelt didn't need money to get me to stop building – all he had to do was have his guys issue violation after violation and shut the building process down completely.

**see: www.whyiwenttojail.com CHAPTER 3 - AUDIO 1**

Later my husband would question Van Pelt about what he had to say to any and all potential buyers. My husband specifically asked Van Pelt what he had said to Greg, who was being called "horsie guy", for the sake of clarity. Van Pelt said that all he told him was that Greg should go around and see what other work my company had done. The audio tapes have Van Pelt saying just the opposite. Here we have Daniel Van Pelt, the Mayor of Waretown, lying to potential buyers and engaging in illegal activity.

My two investigators moved forward with the scheme that Greg was going to buy the Waretown property either as a hole or part even though there were four lots. Greg constantly reiterated to Van Pelt that he was going to use the land for horses. Greg also made it clear that, if he bought the property, he was going to use my company as a builder for the home he was planning to put on the property. Both Ross and Greg seemed to find the right buttons to make Van Pelt and Von Schmidt open up and spill the beans. All of these pleasantries were used to get Van Pelt to talk and see if he was going to give my investigator a price on the property. As if Van Pelt could sell land that I legally owned. On tape Van Pelt offers to look after the property for Greg – he even has the audacity to tell Greg that he would act as the building inspector.

Van Pelt shared with Greg, "I know his reputation as a builder … his story is that he does minimum requirements to get code." Why would any buyer stick around after the local Mayor says something like that to him? My husband and I could only assume that, if Van Pelt was speaking to Greg like this after their first meeting, how many other buyers were turned away by this type of rhetoric.

Ross came over to my house shortly thereafter and said to me that at first he believed that this was going to just be a simple case of one builder against another in regard to codes that couldn't be kept up with. Ross and Greg couldn't believe the stuff they were getting on tape. Here was a Township official bragging about torturing me and bad mouthing my husband. Van Pelt can be heard saying, "He is just an asshole … the MUA is really sticking to him and it cost him $30,000 …Why do you have to be a big jerk all the time? So they tortured 'em." It's one thing to be told something like that, it's another to hear the person saying it, laughing about it. And Mayor Dan Van Pelt was orchestrating all of it. I served two years in prison; I had most of my family walk away from me because of this; this situation destroyed my life – and he thinks it's funny. Another interesting aspect of this conversation is that Van Pelt should have never known about what the MUA was up to. But he did – Collusion?

**see: www.whyiwenttojail.com CHAPTER 3 - AUDIO 2**

On the tapes my investigators even tried to make a deal on a piece of land between mine and Van Pelt's that overlapped a bit. Greg can be heard on the tape discussing how he was going to give Van Pelt a break on the price of the overlapping piece if he is the one to buy the property. Of course Van Pelt didn't turn him down. Van Pelt got about as giddy as a school girl over the idea. On the tapes Van Pelt gives off this vibe that he is untouchable. That he is the master of this little universe called Waretown. As we already know Van Pelt was more than touchable. His arrogance landed a few others in some hot water. His arrogance goes as far as to say that his future plans included naming a shopping center after himself. The shopping center was built; however, it does not bear his name.

In between my investigators meeting Van Pelt near the lot, Van Pelt would be calling my house and mine or my husband's cell phone asking things like if we would move where we were going to build the house on the Waretown lot next to his house. It seemed Van Pelt and his wife had a problem with the fact that we were going to build one house fifteen feet from his property line. Van Pelt's wife wanted our new homes built further away from their land. Greg records Van Pelt saying, "I know his reputation … just wipin' trees out and slapping up [houses]." Gordon Von Schmidt had the same problem and was recorded by my investigator complaining, "We were very upset when this happened … when he split this into four lots … Very unhappy." How come Von Schmidt wasn't "unhappy" with Van Pelt? Greg recorded Von Schmidt saying that "everything up here [Waretown] is acreage … I think the smallest lot is two and half acres. Now everything is rezoned to two acres." Actually the smallest lot was Van Pelt's at under one acre.

To put four homes on that land I was going to have to clear some trees. My husband is recorded as saying to Van Pelt in regards to saving trees, "I'll work with you if you work with me." There was even a discussion about moving certain trees because of their esthetics and beauty. Both Van Pelt and Von Schmidt were telling potential buyers one thing about slaughtering trees when actually the opposite was in the works. Take a look at their properties – Von Schmidt's property is all but cleared of trees. If you look at the picture, Von Schmidt's property was just as wooded as mine. I bet he cleared a couple hundred trees to put in his sweeping driveway and rather spacious back yard. Having my guys clear the trees meant that his privacy was going to be greatly diminished.

**see: www.whyiwenttojail.com CHAPTER 3 - PICTURE 1**

My husband would have more conversations that disproved what Van Pelt and Von Schmidt were saying about him being "not very negotiable" to potential buyers. When Von Schmidt said that, my private investigator, Greg, recorded him later saying, "I've never dealt personally with him, except at meetings … He hasn't appeared very negotiable." Really? If you've never dealt personally with my husband how can Von Schmidt say he's not very negotiable? Also my husband was never at any of the meetings Von Schmidt was speaking of.

Greg continued to ask questions about the property. He knew that both Von Schmidt and Van Pelt were eager to talk. The more Greg talked about how he wanted to turn the land into a horse farm and allow Van Pelt to possibly extend his property line for cheap, the more these guys were willing to open up.

Von Schmidt went into this awesome speech about how the land would look if contoured and cleared the way his mind saw it. Van Pelt was recorded saying, "To me the beauty of the property…is back there." These two guys were on the same page with what they were telling people about the land and my husband.

Von Schmidt told Greg that my husband planned to cut down all of the trees in one particular area. Von Schmidt and his wife were clearly upset about losing their view. "You don't begrudge any builder from making money but … " But what? This statement is all but an admission that these guys were the first wave of torture that I was going to have to endure. Two years of my life were taken away – and part of it had to do with the fact that I needed to cut down a few trees in order to build on land that I legally owned.

At one point Van Pelt called my husband into his office and offered to buy the entire property for $100,000. He wanted us to finance the deal at 2% interest with no money down. Van Pelt was trying to create a sweet deal for himself. Of course we refused. The property in Waretown was worth $800,000, and this guy wanted me to sell it to him for an eighth of its value with an interest rate the US Government doesn't even hand out to first-time buyers. What rules was he playing by?

My refusal to sell the land didn't go over too well with him. The very next day all of our properties were hit with some heavy violations. Van Pelt was recorded saying, "There are rules and if you follow the rules you shouldn't be tortured." My company was complying with every new ordinance the township threw at us. Van Pelt and the town were coming up with new laws almost daily to try and shut us down. Greg got him on tape saying, "Now we're doing new ordinances that you have to maintain 50% of the buffer as trees."

On their next visit to the property my investigators were greeted by Detective Gordon Von Schmidt. Von Schmidt stopped my guy and asked him what he was doing and my investigator told him that he was an interested buyer. Von Schmidt followed suit with Van Pelt and started bad mouthing us. Von Schmidt told Greg that he was at the Board meeting where my properties were being discussed. Von Schmidt went on to say that I should sell the properties for $100,000 or $200,000 less and that I was being greedy. Here were public officials trying to defraud and extort my property from me and I'm the one being greedy. Even though Von Schmidt had never met me or my husband, he was telling my investigator that my husband was difficult to get along with, "that's what a lot of people say."

**see: www.whyiwenttojail.com CHAPTER 3 –AUDIO 3**

Greg went into his story about how he wanted the property for horses and of course Von Schmidt says "that would be wonderful." At nearly the same moment Mayor Van Pelt shows up and continues his tirade about my husband. The second meeting goes no different from the first. Mayor Van Pelt started talking about my bad reputation and then goes on about my husband's bad reputation and how all we wanted to do was just cut down all of the trees. That was when my private investigator offered him that price break as a piece of bait – actually my investigator can be heard just about giving a piece of land away to Van Pelt. Greg was pretending that he may not want all of the property. The Mayor then started talking about other pieces of property in the town. Van Pelt even asked Greg if he could finance the piece of the property that Greg was willing to sell to him with no money down. Again, Van Pelt was trying to get free land.

Van Pelt started talking about how he was buying another piece of land that was directly across the street from mine in Waretown. It was a 12.5 acre piece of land owned by an elderly couple, the Wojciechowskis (wo-jo-how-skees). The torture laid upon these poor people led them to move out of the state.

**see: www.whyiwenttojail.com CHAPTER 3 - AUDIO 4**

## SIMILAR VICTIMS
## THE MAGLIONES

Then there was the Maglione's. Richard and Ginger Maglione were looking for a piece of property in Lacey, New Jersey. They were ready to build their dream home. Rich was a veteran and is an iron worker and Ginger was a freelance respiratory therapist. They found their ideal lot by looking through the tax records in Lacey Township. Previously, they had found a piece they thought was perfect, but were turned away because they were told it was wetlands. I also tried to buy this same piece of property before them. This property sat on a lake right across from a house that I built. The township was adamant that the property was wetlands. Since you can not build on wetlands neither myself nor the Magliones were able to obtain this property. Finally, the Magliones found another lot that they were interested in. This piece of land was part of an estate that was being liquidated by the son of a couple who had recently passed away. What Rich and Ginger didn't know, but were to find out in a harsh way, was that the clerk of Lacey Township, Veronica Laureigh, had previously made a low-ball offer on this property. The clerk wanted to build her own house on a small piece of the property and subdivide the remaining piece so that a very connected builder could build a development on that remaining piece. What made the couple's son sell the property to the Magliones instead, was that he didn't want his parents property sold to a big developer. He wanted someone to build their own home there and nothing more. He even threw in a second piece of property that bordered the original lot for a very good price

What ties the Maglione's story to ours was that this township clerk was and is tied very tightly to the man who runs Ocean County, NJ. Yes, the very same George Gilmore who controls and protects the thugs who stole my property. Right from the start, those that ran Lacey Township made it close to impossible for Rich to build his home which he was doing on his own in his spare time. The building inspector, code enforcer (who happened to be having an affair with the township clerk at the time), planning board, and zoning board worked in unison to make the Maglione's lives miserable. They were forced to go to court repeatedly, where the township's attorneys were paid through the "bottomless pit" that is taxpayer's money. The Maglione's; however, were drained of every penny they had. You don't cross George Gilmore in any shape or form or you pay the price.

At one point, the building inspector showed up at the Magliones' door step after business hours with a police officer. Who ever heard of a police officer coming out for a CO violation. This is part of Gilmore's goon squad. When questioned by Rich later on the phone, as to why he had to bring a police officer with him, the Lacey Township building inspector stated "It was under advisement of the Township attorney, George Gilmore". Obviously it was an attempt to intimidate the couple.

**see: www.whyiwenttojail.com CHAPTER 3 - AUDIO 5**

But, where does the Township Attorney get the authority to make orders like this? It reached a point where the Maglione's were being ordered to pave the entire road that their home was being built on before they could get a certificate of occupancy. Does this sound familiar? The Magliones went to court to challenge this order. Judge Marleen Lynch Ford, whom they appeared before, ruled that the Maglione's only had to pave the part of the road that was directly in front of their home. She told the attorney representing Lacey Township to write up her orders for her signature. That township attorney was our "good friend", Thomas Gannon, the same Thomas Gannon that we had to sue for malpractice for his representation in our subdivisions. What Gannon actually did was write the order exactly how Lacey Township wanted it, and placed it before the Judge for her signature. The Judge signed it believing the orders were written to her specifications. When the Magliones attempted to bring this to her attention, the judge did not respond. When they challenged the order in court, another Judge (who happens to reside in Lacey Township) upheld the forged orders. The Magliones were forced to pay for the paving of the entire road in order to get their certificate of occupancy. Instead of paying $4,400 to pave in front of their home, they paid $22,000 to pave the entire street. This took years of fighting with the Township.

Rich and Ginger decided to bring a Civil Rights suit against the town and hired.... are you ready for this? - Francis Hartman. Just as in our case, Hartman strung them along and then let the statute of limitations run out on their ability to bring a law suit.

Rich and Ginger remained a thorn in the side of the machine that runs Lacey Township (and Ocean County for that matter). At a later point, they got involved in a political campaign. Actually, Ginger signed the petition for a recall election for Board of Education Members. Rich later bumped into the building inspector (at this time the former building inspector) who said to him "I thought you guys were going to stay out of trouble". Rich thought nothing of it at the time. The goon squad would once again be sent after them. Later that week, Rich would come home to find the Lacey code enforcer, John Downing, sitting in his truck up the block from their property. Rich didn't think anything of this; but, the next morning Ginger got in her car and proceeded to drive on the Garden State Parkway. The car was shaking and shimmying uncontrollably. When she got home, Rich found that the lugs on one wheel had been loosened and a few had snapped off. When they brought the car to a local garage, they were told that there was no way those lugs loosened on their own. The mechanic thought it was done intentionally. Downing is the same person who tried to run over and kill my husband on Clearview Street in Lacey. There is a video tape and witness to this incident which we will discuss in a later chapter in the book.

When Rich came with us to meet the Federal Prosecutor shortly thereafter, he told Assistant Federal Prosecutor Joseph Gribko this story. Basically, Gribko looked up at the ceiling and didn't even respond. Rich, in anger yelled, "how would you have felt if my wife's wheel came off and she jumped the barrier and killed someone in your family". Gribko ignored him. Gribko is the prosecutor that put me behind bars and you will learn later how he is connected to George Gilmore.

Oh, by the way, that first piece of property that the Magliones looked at but couldn't purchase because it was wetlands? That's where the Lacey Township Clerk, Laureigh, and this code enforcement official, Downing, had their house built instead. Downing is legendary in Lacey Township for going after people who dare to go against the Town.

I have one friend who wises not to be named in this book. He simply complained about a township police officer's shed crashing into his property every time there was a strong wind. The shed was obviously illegal but the torture that was put on him by Downing because he filed this complaint was unbelievable - endless harassment. There are many others that will not come forward because they are aware of what they will have to endure if they do.

### see: www.whyiwenttojail.com CHAPTER 3 - VIDEO 1

## THE WOJCIECHOWSKI FAMILY

The Wojciechowski family owned a large piece of land in Waretown, NJ; and like myself, they wanted to subdivide the land hoping to make some cash. However the difference lies in that the Wojciechowskis wanted to use the money so that they could move on into their retirement. Their story is integral to mine because it shows a pattern. The pattern it shows will undoubtedly prove that what was done to me was a system that guys like Daniel Van Pelt, like Gordon Von Schmidt and everyone else I will mention used to steal land not just from us, but from many other families in Ocean County New Jersey.

I spent two years in prison for Bankruptcy Fraud and was almost charged with Structuring. I often wonder why the others mentioned in this book were never charged with Collusion, Racketeering and Extortion; because that's exactly what they were doing and had done – not just to me, not just to the Wojciechowskis, but also to the Archdiocese of Trenton, and to many other families in the area including the Magliones, Horner and Ahearn families. I have reached out to some of these families, but none of them wanted to go on the record and risk further reprisals or losses. They saw what happened to me and they did not want to take any chances.

Roseann and Henry Wojciechowski were the only ones who would go completely on the record and supply documents that undoubtedly prove we were all railroaded – starting with the bottom feeders like Van Pelt and working its way up to the very top – US Attorney Chris Christie - now the current Governor of New Jersey.

Roseann Wojciechowski even wrote Chris Christie a letter on August 27, 2008 begging him or a representative from his office to intervene and prevent this atrocity from happening. In the letter she states, 'This is the case of two senior citizens fighting city hall on how the township got their property ... Please attend this trial or send a representative from your office to see how the people of Waretown, NJ are getting scammed on their land." She provided him the docket number and the court date of September 19, 2008. No one from Chris Christie's office ever bothered to attend. Now you would think that a man who has ambitions to be the next President of the United States would seize upon an opportunity to help a couple who have just mentioned that township officials are screwing taxpayers out of their land – especially when that man ran for Governor of New Jersey on the platform to end corruption in the state. What Rose did not realize is that she was probably going to the architect of the plan. Between Chris Christie and George Gilmore they control everything in Southern New Jersey and the fleecing of the Wojchiechowskis was an organized plan.

By bringing up the Wojciechowski family I can prove that I am not someone who is simply *crying* about being wrongfully accused, but proving my claims are true and the methods used against me weren't suddenly cooked up or dreamed up. I am not being paranoid about some far-fetched conspiracy against me that many might say is what this book is all about. As anyone can see, the Wojciechowski family was put through nearly the exact same "torture" I was. The only difference between my family and theirs it that I continued to fight. As Mrs. Wojciechowski put it, "I wish I would've gotten these guys on tape." I did – *that's why I had to go to prison.* Because I had "them" on tape and "they" had no choice but to step up their game against me. "They" had no choice but to make me look like a criminal. If they didn't, more of "them" would be wearing a number and my story wouldn't need to be told.

As the Wojciechowskis will tell you, this fight just wasn't for their land but for their very lives. The health of this elderly couple was put to the test more than once. There was one instance after attending a hearing when Henry Wojciechowski dropped to the floor, suffering from severe chest pains because of all of the stress Van Pelt and his goon squad were putting him under. There was yet another time when Roseann Wojciechowski found her husband on the bathroom floor with his eyes rolled into the back of his head after getting off the phone dealing with yet another issue presented by Van Pelt.

Those reading this book might not understand the severity of the torture that is put upon someone that does not play by their rules. You don't want to answer your door, you don't want to answer your phone, you don't even want to go to your mailbox. It is a 24 hour attack using everything they have in their arsenal, inspectors, code enforcement, corrupt courts all with George Gilmore's appointed judges in Toms River who bend over backwards to do his bidding. They have a proven game plan that they use and they know that if you take them to court, if they don't already own your attorney, the corrupt judges in Toms River will uphold any illegal act that they bring up on a citizen in Ocean County; as the Wojciechowskis soon found out.

As Roseann put it in a letter to the FBI, "my husband is popping nitro like candy". She too suffered from numerous ailments brought on by the stress of this case. The torture laid upon the Wojciechowski family nearly killed them. And I don't mean *killed* in the metaphoric sense, I mean in the very real sense of the word. Thankfully for me, my heart and soul could take it better than theirs could. As for my body, I have a shoulder injury that will never go away. It will always be a constant reminder of my twenty-four months in Danbury, CT.

The Wojciechowski family owned twelve and a half acres of land in Waretown, NJ. Without being subdivided, the land was worth approximately $1.2 million dollars. However, once subdivided this prime piece of real estate could fetch as much as $2.5 million dollars on the open market. These were the numbers the Wojciechowskis were hoping to get. They spent their entire lives on this property and had a wonderful home on this property. Why shouldn't the sale of this land fund their American Dream? Van Pelt and his goon squad had other ideas however.

So, the first thing Van Pelt and his guys did was to rezone the land. The rezoning started at a quarter acre. Then it was raised to half acre zoning. The third time the land was rezoned it went to one acre zoning and finally two acre zoning. The township also doubled the property taxes on the land in "one jump," as Roseann put it. Sounds familiar doesn't it? Just like my 28 acre property in Little Egg Harbor which I discussed earlier.

At one point the Wojciechowskis had a buyer interested in purchasing the land and building houses on it – Van Pelt rolled out the same machine used to scare buyers away from my land. The township, without notifying the Wojciechowskis, moved the zoning to two acres. Out of the blue the potential buyer called them up and said that he was, "backing out of the deal." When asked why, the buyer told the Wojciechowskis that the zoning was now at two acres and there was no way he was going to make any money. For this piece of land one acre zoning was perfect.

The one acre zoning is large enough to put a good-sized home on and leave enough room for a swimming pool and other amenities to be added to the yard. Van Pelt had only ¾ acre and he was able to put an in ground pool and a tennis court on his property. At two acre zoning – no builder can really make money. As Mrs. Wojciechowski put it, "We didn't even get notified … we didn't have a clue." Just like the Wojciechowski's this is the exact same thing they did to me in Little Egg Harbor. There were numerous times when I came home to be completely blind-sided by yet another rezoning or another new set of laws that either held up development of my properties or killed any kind of deal I had with potential buyers.

As one of the legal documents provided to me from the Wojciechowski family states, "By reducing the number of developable sites on the plaintiff's land (The Wojciechowski's), the Township of Ocean substantially lowered the value of the plaintiff's property and a planned deprivation of value without due process contrary to the basic protections afforded the citizens of our Country." Chris Christie could have easily had access to this documentation as well. But, because it was his people that were engaged in this type of behavior, he turned a blind eye – the exact opposite of what he promised the people of New Jersey he was going to do once he took office.

When the Wojciechowskis finally sold the property to US Homes, they hadn't even formally closed yet and US Homes had the deed changed with the township's name on it. Rose has the paperwork that shows the date they filed for the closing and the date the deed was changed … US Homes knew they would be transferring the property … so they just went ahead and changed the name on the deed way before the closing. As the paperwork shows, the Wojciechowskis officially closed on their property on January 27, 2005. It was on January 21, 2005 that US Homes transferred the property to Ocean Township (Waretown) – six days before US Homes even officially owned the property. In any legal sense, this is theft. You can't give away something you don't own.

At the moment the Wojciechowski family realized they were headed for rough water they hired a lawyer, Rich Ramirez, ESQ. He was their lawyer from the very beginning - even before US Homes began stealing their land on behalf of Waretown. This man would turn out to be their Thomas Gannon. Thomas Gannon, was an attorney paid for and hired by me who was actually working for the very same people who were trying to rob me of my land and eventually stole my freedom. If this process only happened to me I can see where some would say I was crying conspiracy theory. However, with the Wojciechowskis starting off with a crooked lawyer and then systematically losing everything – this was a pattern; a proven system; a system they had been perfecting for years. As my tapes prove, they were very proud of what they were doing.

US Homes finally approached the Wojciechowskis with a $750,000 deal. Far less than the $2.5 million it was actually worth subdivided. Remember that question I asked: How did Van Pelt know that once US Homes owned the land that they were going to sign it over to the township. But that's what happened. On the day of the closing, Van Pelt came out of a back room laughing, because he already had the deed to the land signed over to the Township. The Wojciechowskis would later uncover that the deed for their land was drawn up with the Township as owner well before the meeting to sign the paperwork with US Homes. That alone would make anyone wonder what was going on at the County Clerk's office. Just like in my case when Van Pelt wanted part of my land to expand his property, the county clerk had no problem doing what they were told to do and changed his deed to do just that.

Roseann Wojciechowski wrote a letter to "the honorable" Judge Joseph L. Foster of Toms River, New Jersey pleading for justice. Van Pelt had already assumed control of their land prior to any official closing. Mrs. Wojciechowski said, "We didn't have a penny in our hand and they (US Homes) already sold it." But prior to US Homes stealing their land and handing it over to Daniel Van Pelt and the township he controlled, the Wojciechowskis had one chance to get their land back. US homes had put down a deposit on the land. The basic deal behind the deposit was this: US Homes approached the Wojciechowski family and began to engage in a deal for purchasing the land. The Money deposited is so that no one other than US Homes can buy the property. US Homes only had one year to close or they would lose the deposit money. The money would then go directly into the Wojciechowski's bank account and they would be free to sell to another buyer.

This was Roseann and Henry's only chance to regain control of their land – and this chance too would be robbed from them. As I said, Rich Ramirez turned out to be their Thomas Gannon. Suddenly Ramirez started working for the township even though he was paid for his legal services by the Wojciechowskis. He continually refused to hand over the deposit well after the time limit had run out. He even began delivering ultimatums on behalf of the township.

The Wojciechowskis tried unsuccessfully to sue the Township for "Fraud" and "Collusion". As Rose Wojciechowski put it, "We had this little local lawyer … they had a couple of high-powered attorneys – they had the judge [in their pocket] … and I had this little lady who took my case on contingency. We didn't stand a chance. They had unlimited resources … how can you fight them? We didn't have the money to…" At trial, the Judge wouldn't allow the Wojciechowskis anything more than a "yes" or "no" answer during questioning. However, when it came to Van Pelt, he was allowed to speak for as long as he wanted. In addition, the Judge sited Van Pelt's impeccable reputation

When the Wojciechowskis knew they were being ripped off by not only their own lawyer, but from the township itself, they went and got themselves yet another lawyer. In order to fight against Rich Ramirez and the people who paid him off, the Wojciechowskis hired Felicia Russell of Sama & Russell. In order for me to fight against the damage done by Thomas Gannon, I too had to hire an additional lawyer. I hired Fox and Rothschild. Nevertheless, when the Wojciechowskis showed up for their day in court they realized that they were outmatched and out gunned. They had all these lawyers and inspectors and all of these other people present. They were all appointed by the Godfather of Ocean County, George Gilmore. And like Rose said, "all my husband and I had was this little old lady who was now clearly out of her league – we never had a chance. They had unlimited resources … so how do you fight them?" Also, Van Pelt's wife was a sitting judge in the same court house.

In Roseann Wojciechowski's letter to the "honorable" Judge Foster she states, "we did not have a snowball's chance in hell of winning this case. I had a real estate closing lawyer that was ill-equipped to handle this case. She was all I could afford." At that hearing Judge Foster made the Wojciechowskis pay out even more costs in additional appraisals and city planner fees. This is exactly what happened to me only a short period of time later - keep the torture going by bleeding *the mark* dry of all their funds so they get to a point where they can longer fight back. THIS IS A PATERN OF INJUSTICE. Something like this is not supposed to happen in America.

During the hearing the judge stated that the case the Wojciechowskis had brought before him was moot. As the court documents put it, "Plaintiff's complaint is barred as plaintiff's allegations have been rendered moot by the sale of said property to a third party." Of course on this same document there were several other verses of legalese that made sure that the Wojciechowskis would never get justice. I'm not making this up – it's all part of public record. I and the Wojciechowski family can only imagine how well Judge Foster was paid for his services.

How could any one say that there were no third parties involved and that the sale was legal? Anyone with a shred of common sense could see that there were three parties involved: the Wojciechowskis, US Homes and the township. This is collusion – plain and simple.

As Mrs. Wojciechowski tells it, "the judge, during the trial, only wanted me to give yes or no answers." She was basically bullied. As I've shown from the start, the Governor of New Jersey and the US Attorney at the time of all of this – Chris Christie – has used these same bullying tactics against women of all ages – he's still doing it. But don't take my word for it – transcripts from court proceedings are part of public record. They clearly show that the judge in this case, Judge Joseph L. Foster, allowed Daniel Van Pelt to elaborate on all of his answers. And when Mrs. Wojciechowski even attempted to explain what was going on, the judge cut her off. Judge Foster continually stated that he was allowing Van Pelt to speak endlessly because of his "impeccable reputation." Of course Judge Foster allowed Van Pelt to enter into record a string of lies. And yeah, it was Daniel Van Pelt's "impeccable reputation" that landed him behind bars – not for ripping off millions of dollars worth of land from the Wojciechowskis and myself – but for taking a $10,000 bribe from a local scumbag informant – Solomen Dwek.

Also, during the hearing the Judge constantly asked Mrs. Wojciechowski questions that seemed odd or way out of context. Judge Foster asked, "Did you tell Daniel Van Pelt to buy your property?" At first Mrs. Wojciechowski was taken aback by this question. She then realized the context in which his questions were being asked. "I answered that Van Pelt said that my property was worth $1.2 million dollars. Then I said to him, 'if it's worth that much than why don't you buy it?'" And it was this statement that the Judge used to rule in the township's favor. By admitting that she did in fact tell Van Pelt to buy the property, the Judge took it as though she made him an offer, thus eliminating the third party.

Here is this woman, fighting for her land and she makes one sarcastic comment to the person who is clearly trying to rip her off and the Judge makes it look like she is offering the property to Van Pelt. I don't recall ever making any kind of sarcastic remarks on the record, but, those who sent me away certainly twisted the information provided to them in order to make the case against me.

Daniel Van Pelt was successful in devaluing the Wojciechowski's property through rezoning after rezoning. Instead of just pushing buyers away like they did with me, Van Pelt and his goon squad just kept rezoning the land which totally brought down the value. Every time a builder showed any kind of interest in purchasing the land, somehow Van Pelt and company got wind of it and "they" slapped the property with a new set of rezonings.

In my case, not only was I hit with rezonings, but every time a potential buyer showed up that was interested in my land, Gordon Von Schmidt told them how my husband was such a horrible person to deal with and all we wanted to do was cut down all of the trees. Again, I have him on tape – this isn't opinion or hearsay – this is fact. Every time Von Schmidt saw a buyer (my private investigator) looking over my land, he went out of his way to force any and all potential buyers away. Now mind you, this type of behavior is known as collusion. It is a crime. Von Schmidt was a high ranking member of the local law enforcement. If anyone should know that this type of behavior is against the law it should have been him. However, if you are as well connected as Von Schmidt and Van Pelt, what do simple things like the law matter? The Wojciechowskis produced for this book a news article from the Press of Atlantic City that neither my husband or I had ever seen, nevertheless, my husband is somehow quoted as saying, "The laws don't matter down here … They just do whatever they want." Now my husband does not recall ever telling anyone from the press those words, but if he did, they sure state the truth.

US Homes and Daniel Van Pelt ultimately forced the Wojciechowski sale. "So instead of coming out with a million or two, we came out with $750,000," Roseann Wojciechowski told me. I guess this is what Gordon Von Schmidt would say is an acceptable loss as to not look "so greedy" as he said about me to my private investigator. Keep in mind, I have Von Schmidt on tape saying these exact words. I had a construction company; I had a few more resources than an elderly couple looking to retire and this is what "they" did to them.

To add insult to injury, on the final day of the closing there was a major snow storm covering New Jersey. The township, "forced us to pay $1,000 a day for five days to stay," Rose commented, in the home that the Wojciechowskis had owned for decades. This deal – or actually an ultimatum – was set up by the very person the Wojciechowski hired to defend them in court – Rich Ramirez. As Roseann recalled, "They were brutal … It was sell to them or don't sell at all. We didn't have unlimited resources – they do."

"You know what the other kicker was, Van Pelt was able to put a new tennis court on his land … and his land wasn't even an acre." Even local newspapers were reporting on the fact that the new town zoning laws applied to everyone else accept for Van Pelt. Waretown residents were blogging with the intention of hoping to get federal authorities interested in what was going on in Waretown. Again, the ideals that Chris Christie ran on were nothing more than empty promises. During his campaigning in New Hampshire he may have them fooled into thinking he would make a great leader, but back here in New Jersey – we all know differently.

There are many blogs regarding this property. What those blogs were talking about was: At the time the Wojciechowskis were engaged in this battle with the township, their property was zoned at one acre. Van Pelt owned the property next to them. However, his entire property was only three quarters of an acre. He should have never been permitted to build his new tennis court or put in an in ground pool. By law, Van Pelt should have been denied any permits to build anything on his land. That was not the case however. It was exactly what the bloggers were writing about. So, now we have Van Pelt building illegally on his own land; and when the township was engaged in another construction project on land connected to Van Pelt's – wasn't it a coincidence that the same style and type of fencing used in the townships project was now surrounding Van Pelt's land as well. "He's so arrogant he's stupid," Mrs. Wojciechowski said of Van Pelt. A guy like Van Pelt thinks that once he obtains a political office that he is untouchable.

At the end of it, "Your nerves are shot," Mrs. Wojciechowski was speaking about her husband, "I'm not going to let you die for a damn piece of property. The Wojciechowski sold their land to US Homes for $750,000, a far cry less than the $1.2 million it was worth.

The only bit of justice this family was able to get came through an early morning phone call from an FBI agent who had received all of the same evidence presented in this book. During that early-morning phone call, the agent told Mrs. Wojciechowski to turn on the news; and there he was, Daniel Van Pelt being led from his home in handcuffs with a trench coat pulled way up around his ears in an attempt to hide his face. Here was this man in handcuffs who only a short period of time before was standing in a court house smirking at the Wojciechowskis. This was the same man that a sitting judge said had an impeccable reputation. The man who had used every dirty trick in the book to rob these poor people of their retirement was now on his way to jail. Unfortunately, Van Pelt was not being convicted of the crimes he committed against the Wojciechowskis. Van Pelt was set up by Soloman Dwek. Dwek had him on tape accepting a $10,000 bribe.

Mrs. Wojciechowski remembers the day with Van Pelt and all of his "unlimited resources" sitting in the courtroom. And after the judge's gavel had smashed any hope for the Wojciechowski family to receive the retirement funds that they had worked so long for, Van Pelt watched them as they left the courtroom.

At one point in front of Van Pelt's house in Waretown Mrs. Wojciechowski said to him, "You laugh now … but you know what, I'm going to bring you down." Van Pelt laughed hysterically at this and dismissed this elderly woman as though she was nothing more than an insect. Van Pelt treated me and my husband the exact same way. I wish I could say that I received a bit of satisfaction knowing that Van Pelt was heading to prison, but I can't. Someone else just stepped in and took over where he left off in the torture that would continue against me – and it was all because I had them on tape. The ONLY reason Van Pelt went to prison is because I had him on tape.

Mrs. Wojciechowski confessed to me that she wrote Van Pelt a letter while he was serving his time. Part of the letter read that while she lost everything in the end, "You lost your home, your family and your impeccable reputation." There was one final thought that this lovely little old lady who now resides somewhere in Florida wanted mentioned in this book, "If you don't have money in this country you get no justice … if you are an average working-class person you can't get justice because you can't afford it. The judicial system should be for everyone."

At the time my husband and I were listening to the tapes we didn't think anything of Van Pelt's bragging about purchasing this land. It was sometime later after speaking directly to the Wojciechowskis that I was told the true story of the land sale to the Township and Van Pelt. The Wojciechowskis told me that Van Pelt was in bed with US Homes. Collusion anyone?

**see: www.whyiwenttojail.com CHAPTER 3 - AUDIO 4**

# 4. Van Pelt and Company

After all of this, I realized that I had to take certain steps to protect myself, my family and my investments. After hearing their story it is plain to see that Van Pelt and his cohorts were in the business of systematically obtaining smaller parcels of land like puzzle pieces, then packaging them as a single parcel that they would "flip" to well-known large national developers for big dollars. In my case, it reached the point where I could do nothing with the property, so I decided to cut my losses and sell the lots in Waretown "as is". Shortly thereafter, word got back to me that potential buyers were being turned away by "them". Again, because of evidence like these tapes, it was imperative that I be "put away".

Van Pelt and company did the same things to not only this couple and myself – but the tapes revealed that this sort of thing was commonplace. "I don't like our guys sticking it to people because they have a personality problem." If you think about what Van Pelt has said here, it comes across as someone who has just admitted that his guys stick it to people all the time. He didn't like it but he let it happen. The conversation between my private investigator, Greg, and Van Pelt about the Wojciechowskis took place long before US Homes even approached them with any type of deal. Township officials and private building contractors dealing with each other is a conflict of interest – it's COLLUSION! A question that still remains to be answered is: how did Van Pelt know he was getting the Wojciechowski's land for $750,000? He should have never been privy to that information.

Larry Leonard was the Code Enforcement officer in Waretown at the time of my torture. He was yet another official who was making my life a living hell. My husband and I complained to Van Pelt numerous times about him. I have

Van Pelt on tape saying that if it is found that Larry Leonard was "sticking it" to us because of a personality problem, then he would be "written up" for that. Van Pelt knew full well that Larry Leonard was sticking it to us. My husband recorded Van Pelt stating that, "There are certain individuals that Larry has it out for ... and I warned him not to take his personal vendettas out on people on township time." Van Pelt didn't care what names he was dropping or who he was throwing under the bus.

**see: www.whyiwenttojail.com CHAPTER 4 - AUDIO 1**

Even the people at the County Soil Conservation knew Larry Leonard was sticking it to me. I had someone from that office call me because they couldn't understand why I was the only one Larry Leonard wanted fined for not having updated paperwork. There were plenty of other builders who didn't have their Soil Conservation paperwork up-to-date – but I was the only one getting fined for it.

If Van Pelt and company wanted a piece of property and the owners weren't willing to play by their rules, they would rezone the property and hit it with a ton of violations along with a few lawsuits. Just like with me – drain the owners dry of every penny so they can't or won't fight back and then the property can just be taken. And like I said before, Van Pelt and his administrative team were coming up with new ordinances all the time. It made it all but impossible to keep up with all of them. For every new ordinance you have to file paperwork and then there are the inspections. And with Larry Leonard handling my inspections I could expect heavy violations and the costs that go along with them. Extortion.

Like my husband and I, the Wojciechowskis worked their entire lives for the American Dream and here was a pack of "bad dogs" just taking it all away from them after working and saving for so long. "Rose" Wojciechowski once told me that all she wanted to do was, "get out of town. I can't take the *torture* anymore. I didn't want to answer my phone and I didn't want to go to my mailbox." The Wojciechowskis wouldn't face the same incarcerating torture I would receive; but, what Van Pelt and company were doing to them and myself would only be the beginning.

At one point, near the end of my use of private investigators Ross and Greg, I received phone calls from a builder in Lacey by the name of JP Lorton. John Lorton claimed he was interested in my property. This person (Unfortunately we did not tape these conversations. This would be the only time we made that mistake.) claimed to be an interested buyer for my four acre piece in Waretown. He wanted to see how far we would go down in price from the original figures we were asking. When I told this to Ross and Greg, the two of them thought the person we were speaking to was a plant. Turns out my investigators were right. At one point my husband told Van Pelt that Greg, "horsie guy," was no longer interested in buying the land and had disappeared, as was the case with many potential buyers. At one moment they were all "hot and heavy" and in the next minute they were gone without any reason. Van Pelt then asked off the cuff, "You couldn't make a deal with John Lorton?". My husband, a bit stunned, quickly asked Van Pelt how he knew about John Lorton's interest. Van Pelt replied, "I know some people, Rob. I was doing the best I could to market it for you." Is that what he was doing when he and Von Schmidt were making up lies? They were marketing? How many members of the mob or gang members are in prison for the same type of marketing? He was using Lorton as a middleman.

Again, right from the start of my investigation I have Van Pelt on tape saying that Deputy Mayor Robert Kraft was interested in my land. I have Kraft on tape from a phone conversation asking me how much I wanted for the land. Robert Kraft can be heard on tape at a township meeting during roll call refusing to hear the subdivision application for my property. Then he calls me up asking for a price on the land. I guess when my husband and I wouldn't fold like so many others had done in the past – that's when they decided to turn up the heat.

**see: www.whyiwenttojail.com CHAPTER 4 - AUDIO 2**

The same thing that happened to the Wojciechowskis was going to happen to us except the buyer was going to be JP Lorton. Then it became clear to us that this was how they operate in Waretown. This was a major land grab. There was plenty of evidence that the torture laid out on me and the Wojciechowskis was something that had been done in the past and perfected. Another person being tortured was Barry Horner.

## BARRY HORNER AND FAMILY
Barry Horner and his family owned 1,200 acres of land in Waretown since the Revolutionary War. You would think a family with that much history in a town would be rewarded or honored. Nope, the Township came in and as Barry put it, "they cheap-shot us ... in the closing and on the surveys ... there were deed over runs ... where they took over 100 acres," without paying for it. Not all of

Barry Horner's troubles were with Van Pelt. Nope, Barry Horner would be tortured by Van Pelt's predecessor and when these people retired Van Pelt picked up right where they left off.

Barry had a contract on his piece of land for a rather large sum of money to a big developer. Barry has asked us not to disclose dollar amounts as he continues to fight in court for monies owed to him.

Van Pelt can be heard on tape saying that all of the builders Barry planned on using were being turned away. "We turned them all away. We turned all the big developers away." They too were going through all the same types of torture. Barry Horner had state-owned helicopters - tax dollars at work - flying over his land hunting for any violations the township could impose. Van Pelt didn't want large developers building on the land unless he was going to get his fair share of the profit. Van Pelt blocked any attempt by the developers to make a formal Township presentation. Van Pelt even changed the zoning on the land while a contract was in existence. What Van Pelt knew and what Barry would later discover was that there was a clause in the contract Barry had with the developer. If the approval process was halted or difficult, the developer could pull out of the contract. Van Pelt, with his constant rezoning and violations – was causing the delay. Barry even had a high-powered attorney who represented him on another case tell him straight out that he knew Van Pelt was doing his best to block the developer and force them to enact the dissolution clause. Barry also found out that Van Pelt was trying to cut a side deal with the developers. The developers that Barry was hoping to use got tired of the delays and wanted no part in all the lawsuits that were starting to pile up and they backed out of the deal.

Finally, the county came in and offered him pennies on the dollar for the same piece. Barry had no choice but to accept this deal. The township officials that Barry met with told him that if he didn't accept the loss for the land that it would never be sold to anyone and it would be turned into wetlands to prohibit any future sale. To this day he is still trying to get paid for it. Barry let me know of other families who were going through this same type of scam. Van Pelt even had the balls to go after the Archdioceses of Trenton in the same manner. There wasn't a business or a person that he wouldn't do this to. There were so many families, it would take the remainder of this book to list them all. If you tally up the value of all the land that Van Pelt and his crew were grabbing – and this is just what we knew about – it totals more than $50 million dollars from all of the families combined.

# 5. HERE COMES SHORE COMMUNITY BANK

I n late 2004, while all of this is going on with the townships, I was approached
by Shore Community Bank, based in Toms River, NJ. They asked us to give
them the opportunity to assume our land loans and construction loans from
the bank we were dealing with already, Sterling Bank. We had dealt with Sterling for some time. Shore Community Bank told us that they were a local bank
and they would give us a lower rate on land and construction loans on our various dealings and they wanted to keep the money in the community. We were
making money in the community, so why not keep it there. Also, Shore Community told us that they were willing to help us grow our business by financing
projects and loans that outside banks probably would not. What did we have
to lose? We were honest people and we believed that the people at Shore Community Bank really did have our best interests at heart. What we didn't realize
is that this was the first wave from the bigger fish to set me up.

When most people deal with a bank they feel safe. A bank has certain rules
that must be followed; there is over sight to prevent wrong doing. I transferred
approximately 80% of our properties to the care of Shore Community Bank.
Shore lived up to its promises. They gave us a good interest rate. In addition,
Shore made it quick and easy to close on the purchases of properties and construction funding for those properties. We thought things were going smoothly.
We found it a bit odd though, that they were asking my husband to sign off on
all of the loans in addition to my personal guarantee. My husband had no interest in the properties or the business. When the shit hit the fan we realized
why: they wanted to know all of my husband's assets. Those running Shore
Community Bank already knew that they were going to eventually foreclose

on all of these loans. They just wanted a way to tie my husband up in judgments against him. They also asked me to list all of the values of the properties after development. My numbers were going to be much higher than perhaps what a proper appraisal would have been. This is because I was giving them the developed value. But, Shore wasn't looking for any kind of numbers from an appraisal. What they kept asking for was the potential value of the property after it was developed. That's what I gave them. Since I was going to be doing business with Shore, why not tell them all they needed to know. I'm in the construction business not in the banking business. Maybe this information was going to help them maximize my money or perhaps the bank was going to use these numbers to further finance loans. So, being the honest person that I am, I gladly supplied Shore with all of the information they were asking for. Howard Butensky and Joe Mezzina, who I previously mentioned were officers in this bank, had a carefully orchestrated plan for setting us up. This was only the beginning.

While I'm feeling all warm and fuzzy about my relationship with Shore Community Bank and thanking God that at least one thing was going smoothly, all of my properties were getting rezoned. Van Pelt and Von Schmidt were at the height of their torture on me. They were really putting the pressure on every one of my projects. There was nothing we could do to move forward. All of my new construction inspections were failing and construction was being halted because of it. There were bogus excuses thrown about for why we could not get new construction building permits. All of the loans we had with Shore Community Bank were Performance Loans.

Performance Loans are based on time frames. The loan holder sets the amount of time for you to either begin building on your land or get a subdivision. You only have so much time to perform and develop your property. It was no mere coincidence that once Shore Community Bank got 80% of my loans that Van Pelt and Von Schmidt turned up the heat. Also, the heat got turned up in Little Egg Harbor by Mezzina and Butensky. As discussed earlier in the book, this is the same Mezzina of Buena Vista Homes who had a windfall on Nugentown Road in Little Egg Harbor. The paperwork that is involved when land is constantly rezoned takes a lot of time. And since I couldn't get permits and I was receiving wave after wave of violations, the banks wanted to know what was going on. They already knew what was going on; however, because they were behind it. I would have never guessed that the banks would be in bed with the likes of Van Pelt and Von Schmidt.

At one point Shore Community Bank called us into a meeting about the properties we owned. I told Vinny DeLassandro, the bank's representative, that I was having a really hard time getting my subdivisions heard, "The towns are holding us up," I said. That's when my husband and I looked over in the next conference room and there was Howard Butensky. And if Howard was there, Joe Mezzina wasn't too far behind. My husband was shocked to see Howard Butensky. "I'll never forget that day, the door opened up and I turned my head and there he was." My husband almost fell out of his chair. He turned to Vinny and said "what is Howard Butensky doing here?". We had no idea that Howard Butensky was involved with the Bank at this time. Vinny answered that Howard was a board member of the bank. I will never forget that day because this is the point that we knew we were being set up.

As I mentioned earlier, my investigation uncovered that faxes about my subdivision had been passed between Butensky, Joe Coronado, the township's attorney at the time, and Tom Maroldo, the township engineer, before I ever had business dealings with Shore Community Bank. Howard Butensky remains an attorney in Little Egg Harbor and a member of the Board of Directors for Shore Community Bank. But, why in 2002 was he looking into my property? Convenient right? Joe Mezzina runs Little Egg Harbor. He was and remains Chairman of the Little Egg Harbor Municipal Utilities Authority (MUA). So no wonder these two were talking about my property. It was all starting to make sense.

Both Howard Butensky and Joe Mezzina were now going to take a direct role in my torture. The bigger fish had just presented themselves. The bank that I had just begun doing business with out of good faith was now going to be instrumental in putting me behind bars. They had us right where they wanted. They had access to my bank accounts, all of my records – they knew everything. In knowing everything you can manipulate everything ... to fit your needs. Now they had the right to call in our loans – they had control of our subdivisions, they had control of our permits and now they were in control of our loans.

When we sued Thomas Gannon for legal malpractice relating to the Little Egg Harbor and Waretown subdivisions, as soon as we got the settlement check, Shore Community Bank wanted that money deposited in an escrow account in their bank. The bank's representatives, Vinny Delassandro and Dawn Tortola, told us that the officers of the bank wanted to hold this amount in escrow in case we defaulted on any of our loans with the bank. That would be the penalty that the bank would impose on us. In hind sight, this was an obvious attempt to get Gannon's money back to him. As previously stated in the book Joe Coronado, the township attorney, claimed to our attorney, Kevin Thornton of Fox Rothschild, that Gannon is a friend of the town and they wanted to protect him against malpractice. Since Butensky and Mezzina run the town, they wanted to get Gannon's money back to him. I was told by several attorneys that this is illegal for a bank to do. I did not know how Shore was even aware of the suit or the settlement of it as they were not involved with it in any way shape or form. Where would they get this information? This is surely a form of collusion. "They" knew they were going to be able to hold up our subdivisions and then the bank was going to call back the loans. This was how the scam works. They make you feel as though your money is safe with them, all the while they are looking to see if what you have is what they want or perhaps one of their friends wants. Once "they" have you completely under their thumbs all they have to do is begin pressing buttons.

For whatever reason Shore Community Bank wanted my husband's name on all of the land and construction loans that my company had with the bank. My husband was not part of the company and he wasn't taking out the loans. Shore Community also wanted all of my husband's assets tied to the loans. The other thing they asked me to put down on the loans was the value of the property as if it was sub divided and developed. So that's what I did. We didn't realize it at the time. What they were really doing was putting together a game plan to file a lawsuit to use in my indictment.

Later on Shore Community Bank would be a major player in my indictment. Joe Mezzina and Howard Butensky, who run Little Egg Harbor, had our 28 acre Subdivision that they were holding up for no reason. Now we can't move forward on the development of the property and the bank calls in our loans for lack of performance. They are the ones who put the pressure on Joe Sorrentino to raise the taxes on the property so we would lose it. They were in control of everything. There was nothing that we could do. They rezoned our property into five acre zoning. They were looking to hinder the maximizing of the property. Zoned at five acres would allow us to build only five homes on the 28 acre piece. That's why it was so easy for them to turn the property back into one acre zoning which they did shortly after foreclosing on the property. That would allow the new owner to build approximately 27 homes on the 28 acre piece. At 5 acre zoning the costs would be too prohibitive for development to be profitable.

They waited for me to plead to the charges set forth against me as they did not want this evidence to come up in my case. In my indictment Shore

Community Bank was going to testify against me. According to my criminal attorney, Mike Pinsky, had I gone to trial they were going to testify that this property I owned in Little Egg Harbor was worth $5.7 million. That is the developed value of the property. The real value is $299,000 which is what the land is listed for today. That is one of the reasons Pinsky pressured me into taking a plea. The bank also started foreclosure proceedings on this Little Egg Harbor property in 2010 which was suddenly halted for no apparent reason.

Also, in 2010 Shore Community Bank went to court in Toms River and got a judgment against my husband without his knowledge for $1 million, the amount of principal and interest on the various loans they held with my company. So, in the same year the property was worth $5.7 million and then, according to the Bank, worth $1 million. This was kept a secret for almost four years and was served to my husband the week after my sentencing. It had to be kept a secret so that it could not be used to help me at my sentencing. During this time that $1 million judgment that my husband had not been made aware of accrued interest for four years. I could have clearly used this as part of evidence in my case showing that this property was never worth $5.7 million and that it was actually worth the amount that I reported in my bankruptcy filing. But, they sat on it until after I plead to the charges. The property was worth $5.7 million if it could have been developed and I could have sold 27 homes but not as it sat. There was actually no fraud committed on my part. However, they did not want this known. Now that I was sentenced and about to start serving my time, Shore Community started new foreclosure proceedings and took over the properties. That same Little Egg Harbor property is up for sale by the bank now for $299,000 and has been rezoned back to one acre building. $299,000 is a far cry from the $5.7 million the bank would have testified to in the trial against me. Once again, they waited for the appropriate time, after I served my sentence. Also, they rezoned the property back to one acre zoning. The funny thing is that we received notices in the mail informing us that the principal had been paid on this and other properties we owned. When my bankruptcy attorney asked who the mysterious person was who paid the loans he got no response. Whatever money was paid towards the loans should have come off the $1 million judgment against my husband. That is not the case though. He received no credit whatsoever. And we have received no accounting of what payments were made by whom only that payments had been made. We recently discovered that Judge Tranchoni awarded the bank a $1 million judgment but did not connect it to the land or the mortgages on the land. This judge gave the bank a $1 million dollar gift. The question is – what evidence did the bank give that my husband owed $1 million to the bank. Or did judge Tranchoni just do what he was told. The only dealings my husband had with the bank was with the LAND. You see, this ruling lets the bank keep the $1 million dollar judgment and the land and any payments made on the mortgages. Pretty good for the bank, isn't it.

Shore Community knew that they were going to foreclose on the properties. They also wanted to hold my husband up too by filing a complaint and getting a judgment against him. Usually regarding foreclosures the bank will foreclose on a property. After they sell the property whatever is not covered by the income of the sale would become a judgment against the previous owner. Ocean County court let Shore Community Bank do the exact opposite. The court gave the bank a full judgment and, in addition, let them foreclose on the property. This is a win win for the bank. Then mysteriously someone comes in and pays all the principle which doesn't even come off the judgment. That is simply a triple win for the bank. Shore Community Bank got the property, got the judgment against my husband for $1 million and received payment of the principal of the loans from a mysterious party. The bank now owns the property and can sell it for a profit, they have a judgment against my husband and they received full payment on the principal of the loans on the properties.

They were planning this from the very beginning and, since they had very good connected attorneys like Howard Butensky, their plan came off without a hitch. They got the land, I went to jail and my husband was hit with a hefty judgment.

**see: www.whyiwenttojail.com CHAPTER 5 - DOCUMENT 1**

# 6. WHEN I WAS BROUGHT TO THE FBI - THE BEGINNING OF THE END

In late 2007 - early 2008 we were introduced to an attorney by the name of Joseph Bondy. Bondy is located in New York City. Since we had all of these tapes and paper evidence we asked Bondy to help us prepare a civil rights suit against numerous individuals who were in collusion to steal my properties and put my company out of business. After many months of examining the evidence and listening to the tapes Bondy drafted a suit. This suit was never filed however. Instead he reached out to an old colleague of his in the U.S. Attorney's Office, Matthew Skahill. Bondy arranged a meeting for us to meet with Skahill and the FBI in the FBI office located in Red Bank, NJ. Agent Ryan Brogan represented the FBI at this meeting.

Skahill had a level of interest in my case according to Bondy. At the meeting we brought Skahill documents and some transcripts of our tapes. Skahill seemed very interested at the meeting and pulled Mr. Bondy outside to discuss how they wanted to proceed. Skahill was excited because we had Daniel Van Pelt, the then Mayor of Waretown and an Ocean County Assemblyman, and others on tape admitting to my torture and their extortion of my company.

At a subsequent meeting with the FBI and the US Department of Justice held on February 20, 2009 the US Attorney, Ralph Marra, prepared a letter for me and my husband to sign. This letter was supposed to protect us as we were giving evidence to the FBI and would become witnesses if this investigation moved forward. Apparently this is standard procedure in a situation such as this. The paperwork was signed by us and Assistant US Attorney Adam S.

Lurie. As we understood it this document protected us against any possible future indictment against us. We sign a letter to be protected and I am indicted shortly thereafter. Not one person that we brought to the FBI was investigated – not one.

On May 30, 2009 I received an email from attorney Joseph Bondy stating that Mr. Skahill was requesting the original tapes and that this was getting very promising for us.

**see: www.whyiwenttojail.com CHAPTER 6 - DOCUMENT 1**

But, things went quiet. Bondy could not get his phone calls returned from anyone. We were all puzzled as to what was going on. Some months later Bondy found out that Skahill was transferred to a different office. And apparently everyone we met with was transferred. At this point I started to get concerned. Something just did not seem right. As I said earlier, as soon as we began to get comfortable with some one, that some one got transferred out.

After a few months had passed my husband received a phone call from FBI Agent Sean McCarthy. At the time my husband was puzzled because there were law suits that were filed against us and the attorney had the same name, Sean McCarthy. We contacted Joe Bondy because we thought this was some kind of scam. Bondy reached out to McCarthy in the Red Bank FBI office to verify who he was. Sean McCarthy arranged a meeting to sit down with us and go through the evidence. What we did not know at the time is that McCarthy was conducting an investigation for the Federal Prosecutor's office. In fact, there was a sting operation using Solomen Dwek, an FBI informant. This investigation led to a nationally televised arrest of numerous people. All of whom just so happened to be Democrats except for one, Daniel Van Pelt.

We met with Agent Sean McCarthy on two occasions and cooperated with him giving him everything he needed. In addition, we advised McCarthy of other individuals that were going through the same thing as we were. In fact, some of our tapes included conversations about their properties. One couple was the Wojciechowski's who at this point had to move to Florida to get away from the torture. Our tapes revealed collusion between Dan Van Pelt and US Homes to steal this elderly people's Waretown property from them as we discussed earlier.

There was also Barry Horner and his family as we mentioned earlier. Mr. Horner had a large piece of property and he was going through the same thing.

A third meeting was arranged with us, Barry Horner and his son and Sean McCarthy in the FBI Red Bank office. This is when things get very strange. McCarthy is a no show at this scheduled meeting. There was a young agent that met with us, B. Ryan, who was trying to stall for time while he found out why McCarthy was not present. This new agent knew nothing about our case. This meeting became a total waist of all of our time. We walked out of the meeting scratching our heads. The Wojciechowski's also tried to give Sean McCarthy evidence and reach him on the phone; but, like Rose Wohciechowski said, "McCarthy was just blowing me off".

Some time later we received a phone call from Agent McCarthy informing us that the US Attorney has taken over this case, at the time Chris Christie. McCarthy stated that the US Attorney's office had absolutely no interest in our case. But, how could that be? We have taped conversations of torture. We have taped conversations of extortion. We have taped conversations of collusion. We have cancelled checks where the money is missing to this day. And the Federal Attorney, Chris Christie, who was supposed to be so big on corruption, has no interest. After a lot of yelling by us and other residents whose property was being stolen from them we were put in touch with Tom Mahoney, an agent and investigator in the US Attorney's office.

We contacted Agent Mahoney who was about as nasty to us as anyone could be. It was like we were bothering him. Mahoney finally agreed, just to shut us up, for us to email him some of our evidence. We sent him what was requested of us and we never heard back from Mahoney. None of us who were involved in the land grab could get anywhere with Mahoney. You had Ocean County residents, just the ones we know about and apparently there are many more, who lost over $50 million worth of properties to these corrupt politicians and officials. And Mahoney wants to know none of it. Apparently at this point, after listening to our tapes, they knew Van Pelt was an easy target and he liked to talk. The FBI had set up a sting using informant, Solomen Dwek, to get Van Pelt to take a bribe of $10,000 for selling his influence with the DEP to get wetlands overlooked. This sting was very successful. Dwek was able to get Van Pelt in a meeting where Van Pelt accepted a $10,000 bribe. And this is all Mahoney cared about – that they have Van Pelt on a $10,000 bribe. We had $50,000 worth of checks missing. $30,000 of it is discussed on our tapes. And to this day this money is unaccounted for. And Mahoney is only interested in this $10,000 bribe?

A gentleman who has been trying to help numerous residents down here by the name of Barry Bendar called up Mahoney and got into an argument with him. Barry Bendar was the Democratic Chairman in Lacey Township who had numerous people come to him for help in similar situations on land issues. Agent Mahoney did not want to hear anything. He told Bendar that this is not a federal problem. Mahoney said that this should be brought to the Ocean County prosecutor. So, let's see – you have all of these public officials and local politicians in collusion with each other and some are the ones who appoint the Ocean County prosecutor and this is where he wants everyone to go for help.

Months earlier I brought our evidence to the Ocean County Prosecutor's office. We never heard back from them. Soon thereafter the most vicious attack on my family began. And this is who Mahoney wants us to go back to. You have to be joking. At this point the authorities came after my son, not once but twice. My husband's Social Security disability was pulled and they claimed he owed all of the money he was paid back from 1997. To this date he still cannot get a hearing or copies of his file. It must be hidden with President Obama's birth certificate. My family's health care was terminated. I was indicted and the federal and state IRS was sent after us. The police stop us constantly for no reason. In fact, my young daughter gets pulled over by the local police no less than 15 times a month. We even get citations on my two little dogs who never leave the house. As of the writing of this book, the attacks on my family just do not stop.

You must understand, at the time we did not realize that we were complaining about an area which is controlled by Chris Christie's friends. In fact, we were later told that even Tom Mahoney is a good friend of Christie's and was appointed by him. One of the township attorneys who has tremendous influence in the towns is Gregory McGuckin, a very close friend of Christie and his college roommate. (In the recent Bridgegate investigation isn't it ironic that Christie was investigated by Mahoney and McGuckin.) And the town we were having most of our trouble in, Waretown, was where Chris Christie's father, Wilbur Christie lived. Wilbur moved shortly after Van Pelt's indictment. And this is all looked over by yet another friend of Christie, the godfather of South Jersey – the person who appoints everyone to every position – George Gilmore – the republican chair.

# 7. GEORGE GILMORE

So, who is George Gilmore and what is his relevance to this story? The website PolitickerNJ had this description in their 2014 Power List of political players of their #4 most powerful entity:

"Easily the most powerful GOP chair in the state, ruler of New Jersey's biggest and most important Republican county and simultaneously a principal at 1868, one of the state's most potent government affairs firms, Gilmore has put together an impressive winning streak focused on executive offices. He was a primary financial backer of the mayoral campaigns of Don Guardian in Atlantic City (2013) and Jose "Joey" Torres in Paterson earlier this year. He also racked up a strategic win with the stemming of movement conservative Steve Lonegan in the CD3 GOP Primary and the convincing general election victory of Republican Tom MacArthur. One thing is clear: any Republican running for statewide office must go through Ocean"

The only ones that rated higher in their list were #3, George Norcoss, the political boss of the Democratic Party, #2 Independent PACs (not even a person), and #1, Paul Fishman, the Federal Attorney for NJ, whom Gilmore has operatives working for (see previous comments about Joseph Gribko), that Fishman refuses to "weed out"

When they state "ruler of New Jersey's biggest and most important Republican County", they mean it literally. Gilmore is the man with the ultimate power, and he loves to "micro-manage".

As stated in an Asbury Park Press story dated August 21, 2007, " Gilmore is head of the Ocean County Republican Party and one of a dozen or so unelected political bosses who determine, in large part, what happens in state and local governments in New Jersey."

Again, from the same story , "His fund-raising prowess, political savvy and connections in Trenton and Washington, D.C., have made him perhaps the most powerful politician in the county."

"George is a formidable opponent," said Jack Moriarty, former president of the Dover Township Democratic Club, who has been the chief campaign strategist for Dover Democratic campaigns for the past three years. "His power and control over the money and appointments in Ocean County mean that he is unquestionably the man in charge of everything."

That power is again delved into later in the same story; " In late 2001, Gilmore again came under fire when he worked with GOP Assemblyman James W. Holzapfel to have Republican Thomas F. Kelaher appointed Ocean County prosecutor and the Republican prosecutor, E. David Millard, Holzapfel's former law partner, elevated to a Superior Court judgeship.

Yes, this is the very same Judge Millard referred to earlier in this book, and you can plainly see that he still follows Gilmore's orders to the hilt. We've been told that judges in Ocean County do not get appointed without Gilmore's "nod".

Gilmore's notoriety goes back to the Reagan years, when he and Larry Bathgate were big fundraisers for the President. And yes, this is the same Larry Bathgate that Solomon Dwek was pursuing when Federal Attorney, Chris Christie "blew a gasket" over it per Lou Manzo's book.

Gilmore's influence in Washington D.C. is clearly spelled out by this blurb from a 2006 Press Release from President George W. Bush's office, for the First Lady. This is a short piece from a speech she gave at the June 13, 2006 Fundraiser for Senate Candidate Tom Kean Jr.:

> "I also want to acknowledge your former governor, Christie Todd Whitman — Governor Whitman. Thank you so much for being here today. (Applause.) And our friend, Larry Bathgate, your host today — Larry, and George Gilmore, thank you both very, very much."

Knowing that Chris Christie was appointed Federal Attorney of New Jersey by President George W. Bush, and Gilmore's "close" relationship with the Bush family as a political fundraiser, it would not be a surprise that Christie obtained his position of great power at Gilmore's urging, despite his lack of qualifications and experience. When Christie defeated the sitting NJ Governor Jon Corzine by the smallest of margins, he openly thanked George Gilmore for "delivering" Ocean County's votes. The question in the back of my mind is, were these votes delivered through fundraising, or did it have something to do with his position as Chairman of the Ocean County Board of Elections?

In Ocean County, the firm of Gilmore and Monahan was paid over $19 Million dollars in taxpayer dollars by Government entities at all levels between 2006 and 2014, over $16 Million of which came from Ocean County Municipal Governments, School Boards, and Municipal Agencies.

The appointments by these entities in Ocean County are made by officials elected via donations from Gilmore's firm and associated PACS among which is the large GOPAC fund, which he serves as director of, with votes counted by the Ocean County Board of Elections, again, headed by George Gilmore. Seems like a very "symbiotic" relationship, doesn't it? The saddest thing is that those charged with enforcing the law, turn a "blind eye" to this obvious conflict of interest, including the Democratic leadership in Trenton.

In regard to law enforcement, how can we expect the Ocean County Prosecutor's Office to question anything Gilmore does? It is currently headed by "our good friend", who is previously referred to in this book, Joe Coronato, who's appointment and power can be directly attributed to George Gilmore. Coronato's predecessor, Marlene Lynch Ford (as in the Maglione's) , a former Democratic Assemblywoman, was first appointed a judge (I'm assuming with Gilmore's "nod"), then stepped down from the bench to become the Ocean County Prosecutor when Tom Kelaher, the then Ocean County Prosecutor, was pressed into service as Mayor of Toms River, replacing then candidate Greg McGuckin (yes, our Greg McGuckin) due to the disclosure of McGuckin's failure to pay over $121,000 dollars in Federal Income Tax. Then Ford was re-appointed a judge when Gilmore wanted "his boy" Coronato to be the Prosecutor. This see-saw activity points out the absolute power Gilmore yields over both Political Parties in Ocean County. The Democrats march to his beat also.

At the higher levels of Law enforcement, the State Attorney General is an appointment of Chris Christie. So obviously any wrong doing by Gilmore would be invisible to them, and in the Federal Prosecutor's office, you have Christie's operatives like Gribko and Mahoney, who's activities are either ignored or condoned by Democratic Federal Prosecutor, Paul Fishman. Is it any wonder that nothing ever becomes of "shenanigans" pulled by Gilmore as listed below, despite public outcry:

Michael Rittaco was indicted and convicted of taking "kickbacks" from a insurance firm in his position of Superintendent of Schools in Toms River. The Law firm that represented the School Board at that time was Gilmore and Monahan. Nothing was ever asked about their possible involvement.

As reported in PolitickerNJ, "McGuckin makes millions from his political connections, and helped all time pay-to-play champ County Boss George Gilmore corrupt the Off Track Betting Parlor application in Toms River so the public never got any real input. Gilmore got huge fees for representing the gambling interests, and McGuckin's wife got a useless $90,000 "job" at the County Election Board where Gilmore is the chairman.

Then there was the scandal regarding the cleanup in Ocean County following Superstorm Sandy. As reported by the Star Ledger of Newark, NJ, "Gilmore, the Ocean County GOP chairman and one of the most powerful players in state Republican politics, confirmed yesterday that he was hired by AshBritt. He declined to say what his role is or address whether he avoided conflicts of interest due to his other role as attorney for towns, including Seaside Heights and Jackson Township, that used the firm. "Due to a confidentiality clause, I cannot comment," Gilmore said. AshBritt's Moskowitz declined to answer a question about Gilmore. AshBritt is not the only debris removal firm linked to Gilmore. State records show Gilmore registered as a lobbyist and lobbied the governor's office for the DRC Group, a debris removal firm from Alabama that was looking to secure a state contract.

"That wouldn't be a surprise me," Drewniak said. "We hear from so many registered lobbyists from New Jersey, so I couldn't immediately say what the discussion was about."

Along the lines of Superstorm Sandy, there was the inordinate amount of Storm relief money that went to the Boardwalk at Seaside Heights, routed there by Governor Chris Christie. It just so happens that George Gilmore has very close ties to Seaside Heights, having grown up there, and whose Grandfather, J. Stanley Tunney served as Mayor there for 25 years. Gilmore's interest in the Saw Mill Bar, which is on the Boardwalk, is documented in a 2004 Asbury Park Press story, relating the beating of Kevin J. Kopacko at the hands of Seaside Park Police on June 6, 2004, supposedly for his video taping of their activity outside the Saw Mill. From the story; "Kopacko made the video because his boss, Sawmill owner Stephen D'Onofrio, and D'Onofrio's former lawyer, George R. Gilmore of Toms River, had instructed him to visually document the activities of the police officers who routinely gathered outside the Sawmill at closing time."

Obviously, Gilmore has close ties to the Boardwalk, but long after the Superstorm had passed and caused it's damage to the Boardwalk, there was a fire (due to inadequate wiring, we're told) that damaged another portion. Again, even though this fire had nothing to do with the Storm, Federal relief funds were used to make the repairs. Chris Christie made sure his benefactor, Gilmore was well taken care of. In the mean time, there were hundreds of Ocean County residents still homeless, and waiting for these Federal funds to help rebuild. I'm sure they enjoyed watching Christie make a spectacle of himself on television, hovering around Seaside Heights as the Boardwalk burned.

In the March 11, 2015 story in the Paterson Times, it was reported; "Gilmore's law firm, Toms River-based Gilmore and Monahan, received a $100,000 contract to handle state and federal cases for the city.

Partners from some of the firms were present before council to take questions. Thomas Monahan, Gilmore's partner in the law firm, was asked whether his firm had worked with a large city like Paterson, by Kenneth Morris, councilman at-large. "We have not, but the law is the same," responded Monahan. Monahan said the firm presently represents eight Ocean County municipalities including East Brunswick and South River. He also said the firm represents the South Jersey Transportation Authority and the Atlantic City Expressway.

Morris asked Monahan's firm in certain instances suggested policy changes to municipalities that would better protect them against litigation. "We have," said Monahan. He said in one instance his firm suggested policy changes based on a court case to a municipality.

Gilmore's firm received its first city contract yesterday evening. Gilmore was instrumental in securing Torres the business administrator position in Jackson Township after he was defeated by former mayor Jeffery Jones. "

As reported in the Asbury Park Press on September 7th, 2007, both George Gilmore and then Toms River Council President Gregory P. McGuckin (now State Assemblyman in the 10th Legislative District of NJ) had Federal tax liens placed against properties they owned for failure to pay income tax. McGuckin was a candidate for Mayor of Toms River at the time and, as mentioned earlier, he later dropped out to be replaced by former Ocean County Prosecutor, Tom Kelaher. McGuckin owed more than $121,000, while Gilmore was delinquent to the tune of $158,716. I would think that someone who was less politically connected than Gilmore and McGuckin would have done some "hard time" for such an oversite.

As things went, this story was reported once, and was never heard about again. This is the standard for "problems" that crop up for Gilmore and his minions.

In a PolitickerNJ story reported on September 18th, 2007 (around the same time as the Income Tax revelations), Richard Strada (the then Democratic Candidate for Mayor of Toms River) requested the State Attorney General's Office, and the U.S. Attorney's Office investigate the proposed purchase of property formerly known as the Albocondo Campground by the Toms River Board of Education. Strada said in a release: "The fact that (Ocean County Republican Chairman) George Gilmore represented Sandcastle, L.L.C. who bought the property just last year for $3 million dollars and is now poised to sell it for $7.7 million dollars to the school board whom Gilmore also represents sets off alarm bells." The property in question when sold to Sandcastle was slated to provide 45-acres of open space along the Toms River for public enjoyment while allowing the construction of senior housing on a portion of the tract. "Mr. Gilmore's financial relationship to this tax-payer funded transaction and to those who stand to profit from it should be disclosed and scrutinized by law enforcement agencies" stated Strada, who served as Mayor in the 1970's.

The Strada campaign is concerned by what appears to be a pattern of ethical improprieties involving GOP boss Gilmore. "Last week it was his failure to pay income taxes; this week it's insider land deals at the taxpayers' expense. It's incredible that the School Board continues to retain his counsel amidst these scandals," Strada said. These statements were made far before the Rittaco indictment.

Now, to bring Gilmore's influence directly to my story, you will recall that the initial meeting between Dan Van Pelt and Solomon Dwek took place in George Gilmore's Toms River Office, with Alphonse Santoro (the long time Ocean County Democratic Chairman) and George Gilmore in attendance. It is mentioned in Lou Manzo's book that Van Pelt stated he was "ordered" by Gilmore to attend this meeting. I've been told by Ocean County Political insiders that Van Pelt was never one of Gilmore's favorites, and that Gilmore actually wanted Lacey Township Republican Boss, Gary Quinn to get the 9th Legislative district Assembly seat, but it went to Van Pelt in a power struggle (that Gilmore later took care of in the 2010 election, eliminating the competition).

It was this meeting that initiated Van Pelt into becoming the only Republican to be caught up in the "sting" initiated by then U.S. Attorney, Chris Christie. Initially, this "sting" was to be used to discredit and dismantle the Hudson County Democratic organization, clearing the way for Christie to "stroll in" as Governor of NJ. Then why would he change direction and target a Republican Mayor in

Ocean County? As reported by NJ.com, it was found in Alphonse Santoro's testimony in an FBI document that he was told by George Gilmore prior to the final "round up" of Bid Rig III, as Christie's "sting" became known, that he (Gilmore) heard about the arrests. Here is the excerpt from NJ.com; "Santoro advised that approximately one week prior to the July 23, 2009, Federal Bureau of Investigation (FBI) raids, he was told by Gilmore that there was going to be a lot of arrests north of the Raritan," an FBI summary of the interview says. "Gilmore did not provide any more details and did not say who told him." The document was one of several made public after former Assemblyman Lou Manzo sued the U.S. Attorney's Office, claiming discriminatory prosecution.

Gilmore's organization is credited with boosting turnout in heavily Republican Ocean County to help elect Chris Christie governor. It was Christie who initiated the investigation that led to 46 arrests.

Gilmore told The Auditor he had heard rumors of a raid, but not from Christie or anyone in the U.S. Attorney's Office.

"All I know is what I was told. ... There was going to be a whole bunch of indictments," Gilmore said. "I got no inside information. I didn't talk to any law enforcement official of any type with regard to that. Someone had mentioned it to me and I just said it as an aside."

When a Christie spokesman, Michael Drewniak, was asked if his boss, no longer U.S. attorney when the raid came, knew it was coming and, if so, did he tip off Gilmore, he said, "Oh, for goodness' sake. Absolutely no and no."

When my Husband and I began communicating with the FBI in Red Bank, NJ, we signed documents to protect us as we testified against the corruption we were victims of. We turned over all of our tape recordings implicating Van Pelt and crew.

**see: www.whyiwenttojail.com CHAPTER 7 - DOCUMENT 1**

We thought we were safe, but when Gilmore and Christie got wind of the recordings, they needed to do something. Again, how would it look for Christie, a candidate for Governor of NJ, to have one of his best friends (Greg McGuckin) indicted for his involvement in the "land grab" that was going down in Ocean County, and to have his Father living in the town (and involved with the Republican Party) in the town where most of this was happening. And for Gilmore, it was an excuse to get rid of a "big mouth" whose own self value caused issues for the Ocean County Boss. My thoughts on this were that Gilmore, not only knew

71

of the "sting", but was a participant in it. I believe that initial meeting in his office was a pre-orchestrated set up, that Dan Van Pelt never had a chance to escape. And, as I mentioned earlier, Van Pelt was treated with "kid gloves" as to not have him "spill the beans" on the level of corruption being perpetrated in Ocean County by Gilmore and his mob. With Van Pelt out of the way, Gilmore had a clear path, through his law enforcement connections, and corrupt attorneys, to discredit me, and have me sent to prison for two years.

# 8. VAN PELT HAS TO GO

It took me a little time to figure out what was going on exactly. Christie was about to run for the Governor's office. Agent Sean McCarthy and his informant, Solomen Dwek, were taking down Christie's enemies. That is why all of the people in the sting were democrats – I believe there were 43 of them and 42 of them were democrats. To set up Van Pelt during the sting, Van Pelt was ordered into George Gilmore's office by Gilmore himself. They wanted Van Pelt present at the meeting with Solomen Dwek. But, they would like you to believe that Gilmore had no idea who Solomen Dwek was. There has been two books written on this subject, (The Jersey Sting) and (Ruthless Ambition - the Rise and Fall of Chris Christie). These two books just assume why Van Pelt was taken in, the only republican. No one knew about me and what we brought to the FBI. I hit too close to home. You had a lower henchman, Van Pelt and his boys, doing a lot of the dirty work down here and being rewarded by being moved up the ladder slowly and given numerous jobs in agencies.

They had a problem now, however. Van Pelt liked to talk. He liked to brag about how powerful he was in a small town. He even told my private investigator how he met Secretary of State, Dick Cheney. I was naïve. I thought I was going after a small politician who was abusing his power for his own financial gain. I was so wrong. This went all the way to the top. When Skahill was shipped out they had to bring people in to stop my investigation. That is why Sean McCarthy and Tom Mahoney were brought into the case. They needed people that would play ball with them. Christie was running to be Governor and how would it look for an investigation to become public that would indict his friends and be in a town where his father lived. Waretown was very

73

proud of the fact that they had the Governor's father living there and they were very vocal about it. Also, Christie had to protect their friends.

On February 19, 2015 David Sirota of the International Business Times reported a story about Bennett Barlin, a Hunterdon County prosecutor, who indicted approximately 30 of Christie's friends. Christie asked him to back off and when Barlin refused he was simply fired.

There was another incident documented in Manzo's book, where Solomon Dwek was setting up a prestigious lawyer, Larry Bathgate. As written in Ruthless Ambition, Christie placed a phone call to Sean McCarthy to call his dogs off this lawyer. This is why so many law firms sell out their clients in New Jersey. If lawyers don't do what Christie requests of them they get the dogs after them. But, if you are a firm that plays by Christie's rules, you are protected. This is one of the reasons I had so many attorneys not show up in court for me and they were willing to face malpractice charges because of it.

They now realized that they had to get rid of Van Pelt. But, they had to do it in a way that wasn't too harsh. They did not want him talking. And if they gave him too long of a sentence this would probably happen. That is why they only wanted to know about the $10,000 bribe. Van Pelt's wife, who was a sitting judge in Ocean County, was never brought into the situation even though she was in the meetings with Solomon Dwek. Soon after his indictment, I got phone calls from numerous real estate friends informing me that Van Pelt's house located in Waretown went on the market for approximately $630,000. The market had just crashed, however. His house was worth maybe $400,000 in a good market. They were all laughing thinking it was ridiculous – no way could this house be sold never mind get appraised by the bank in one of the worst real estate markets since the great depression. However, it only took a few days and the house was sold for cash. The joke was on us. NO appraisal needed with cash real estate sales. Everyone who informed me was stunned. But, I knew what was going on. Take a $10,000 bribe charge, get double market value on your house which there was almost no mortgage on, don't involve your wife who is a sitting judge and keep your mouth shut. This is something straight out of a movie – isn't it? There was only one thing left AND THAT WAS TO DEAL WITH ME. Make me and my family so toxic that no one would listen to us.

# 9. HOW THEY GOT ME INDICTED

A friend of ours who was also a neighbor, Ernie Olivera, told us about an investment company located in Lacey, NJ. His brother in law worked for this company that was called Global Trading. It was owned and operated by Brian Winters. I was asked if I would like to invest in the company. Most of our neighbors were investors and we were given references of local businesses that also invested. In fact, some were invested with Global for several years. I spoke with many of these investors. One of the companies I spoke to was right down the street from my house called Barnegat Tree Service. The owner of Barnegat Tree Service told me that he made $80,000 on a small investment in only one year. He said he was dealing with Global for some time and he felt that they were straight up. So, after talking to these people and trusting Ernie, over the next year or so I also invested some of my money. My mother in law and my accountant also invested after doing their own investigation of the company.

Initially we had no problems with Global. When we sold a property we would deposit some of the proceeds into our Global account. When I needed cash to purchase land I liquidated some of my funds to purchase the land. There were no problems in the beginning of my dealings with Global. There came a time when I needed to make a land purchase and I was unable to get in touch with Brian Winters to liquidate some of my holdings for the purchase. He was not returning my calls. I had to hire attorney Glenn Stern to contact Winters and threaten him to liquidate my holdings and withdraw my funds. At this point I felt uncomfortable with Global and started calling people I knew who were also investors with Global and telling them that something was just not right with Winters and his company. I even called Ernie Oliviera to ask his brother in law what was going on and Ernie defended Winters. It turns out later that he was working for Winters and apparently receiving a commission on people that he was bringing into the company. With the assistance of Glenn Stern we were able to get a good portion of my money out that was said to be in my account. At this point I was just happy to be ahead of the game and never pursued the balance which was in excess of $100,000.

Shortly after this I was told from people that I knew that Global Trading was dissolving and that they could invest in a new corporation called Wynham Goup which was also owned and operated by Brian Winters. At this point I was out. I was no longer an investor. I told my mother in law when she received one of these notices to take her money and get out. Also, we told friends that we knew who also got these notices to take their money and get out because of the problems I had and that I had to get an attorney to get my money. None of them took our advice. It's funny – people only remember that you told them about this company. But, when I told them that things did not seem right and I had to get an attorney they still rolled their money into the new company and eventually lost it.

A couple of years later I received a call from a gentleman by the name of Rudolph Basserman. Basserman was from the Bureau of Securities. On the call I was informed that an investigation was being launched against Global Trading and Brian Winters. Basserman suggested that I come to his office in Newark, NJ for questioning. At this time I have yet another attorney, Kevin Thorton from Fox and Rothschild. Thorton contacted Basserman about the investigation. Basserman assured my attorney that he doesn't need to be at the questioning because all Basserman intended to do was question me about Global Trading and Brian Winters. Basserman also assured my attorney that I was not under investigation in any way. Was Thornton just an incompetent attorney or was he part of the set up? Remember he worked for a very distinguished firm in New Jersey, Fox and Rothschild, who has many political connections in the state. You would think Thornton would know better and protect his client. I attended this meeting in good faith and answered all of the questions Basserman had to ask. However, at this meeting I was suddenly blindsided. Basserman began to show me forged mortgages and checks with my signature that I had no knowledge of. These were signed documents that he obtained during his investigation of Brian Winters.

I was later sued by the bankruptcy trustee for Global Trading, Eric Perkins, for the money I received from my investments. My husband was sued also even though he never had an account with Global. They also brought criminal charges against me because when I could not get my money out of Global I hired attorney Glenn Stern to help me get my money, and they claimed that I knew Global was a ponzi scheme. I hired yet another lawyer, Joseph Casello from Manasquan, NJ . Casello read the complaint and examined my information and he assured me that I had nothing to worry about. I had heard that before. Casello would turn out to be another attorney who was either influenced by "them" or totally incompetent. Casello filed the answer to Perkin's complaint late and once more I made the mistake of being out of town when Casello went to the hearing with the judge. Casello lost the case in summary judgment which means that there was no disputed facts to be argued on my behalf; therefore, there is no need to go to trial.

In bankruptcy court Judge Lyons awarded the trustee $243,000 from me and $243,000 from my husband. How could that be? My husband didn't even have an account with Global Trading so how could a judge impose such an award? After arguing with Casello upon my return that the judge's numbers were wrong and why didn't he fight that my husband didn't even have an account, Casello went back to Lyons and argued those facts. Lyons changed his ruling to $343,000 against me and $30,000 against my husband. This is the first time Judge Lyons had to change his ruling because of phony evidence presented to him. How could he award $343,00 against me when they were only suing me for $243,000 and how can he award $30,000 against my husband when he never had an account with Global? At that point Judge Lyons should have sent this case to trial because he knew he had phony evidence. Casello asked the judge to be relieved as my counsel. He told the judge that I owed him a substantial amount of money. I paid this man tens of thousands of dollars and he said that I owed him less than $2,000 that I was not even billed for. Now he is requesting to be let out the case at such a late date. I would later discover that Casello's wife was a clerk in the same bankruptcy court as the judge who was hearing our case. The judge didn't know that?

I went on to seek out another attorney who could effectively represent me in the criminal suit. I met with many attorneys, however, none were interested in taking over a case that had been screwed up so badly by Casello. Every attorney that I met with advised me that no judge would recuse an attorney when their client had an upcoming criminal case in less then 2 weeks. They also said that this is a major malpractice on Casello's part and they did not want to get involved with such a case. Again, he was either working for "them" or he was totally incompetent. Each attorney I met with asked me the same question "why are they going after you so hard?". "You are a small piece of the puzzle", they said. "You only received $243,000. Global was a 20 million dollar company so why were they only going after you and no one else." "It will cost them more to go after you then they would get back from you." It didn't make any sense to them. What they did not understand is that they wanted me punished for going to the FBI. This was not a normal case. Also, Global's trustee had money in their account to return to investors that they recovered from Brian Winters. They were not going to let that happen. They wanted that money for themselves. What was the best way for them to grab that money for themselves – to bill more legal hours because the investors can only get back what the lawyers did not spend. So you can bet they were going to spend every cent. This left me with no other option. I had to go to trial and represent myself as it pertained to good faith in the criminal suit.

Because he was charged my husband had to hire an attorney. He was advised by this attorney that it was cheaper to pay the $30,000 judgment they had against him than to keep spending money on legal fees. At the advise of my husband's attorney, he paid the $30,000 plus interest to take him out of the law suit. However, and this is where things really began to get crazy, the trustee refuses the payment and returned the certified check to him. If someone has a judgment against you and you pay that judgment in full they must accept the payment and discharge you from the case. So, why wasn't anyone upholding the rules of law? Why wasn't Judge Lyons forcing the trustee to follow the rules of law? The judge that sentenced me for my indictment, Judge Freda Wolfson, insisted at the sentencing that my indictment case was all about getting money back for the Global investors that lost money. If that was the case, why didn't they accept my husband's $30,000 payment? Attorney Heilring, who represented the trustee, wrote to Judge Wolfson informing her that he was trying to recover moneys for investors. None of the original people I talked to who invested in Global before me were even contacted to give their money back. I know two people that received substantial returns on their money and they were never contacted to return any funds. Later it would be discovered that my husband didn't owe anything.

Also, at my sentencing hearing Judge Wolfson and Gribko portrayed me as a sophisticated criminal in how I moved money around my several bank accounts. I am not a sophisticated criminal. If that were the case I would have just left the money in the corporate accounts where it could not have been touched. I simply did what I was advised to do by forensic accountants that I trusted at the time.

After Judge Lyons set forth the summary judgment, my husband and I were called in for depositions with the trustee. My husband should not have had to be there but they were breaking every rule in the book and they were getting away with it. To attend the deposition with us we hired attorney Andre Kydala. The day of the deposition Heilring walked into the room and asked Kydala if he could speak to us off the record. Heilring proceeded to yell and curse at us while Kydala just sat there like a puppy dog. Heilring threatened us, my family and friends. He said that he would go after everyone we knew and that he would make our lives miserable. The line that stuck out the most is that he said that Judge Lyons was on board with them and that the Judge would do anything they wanted him to do. From what I had seen so far – I knew this was true. What attorney just sits there and lets their client go through this. Kydala never got up to object. He did nothing. It was as though he was scared because he knew Heilring was so connected. Later on he wrote letters to the judge because we forced him to. I discovered in the deposition that Joe Casello ordered a title search on me by a title company that his firm uses and he handed this search to Heilring. Why would my own attorney do this? Why would he purposefully try to hurt me? This is a similar circumstance as the one I mentioned earlier regarding attorney Klingerman. Klingerman intentionally gave Heilring's firm privileged information about my husband's assets. Why were my attorneys bending over backwards to help this law firm? Probably the answer, which you will see later, is that their connections go right up to the US attorney's office. Who was sitting there at the time, Chris Christie.

In late 2005 I hired attorney Francis Hartman located in Haddonfield, NJ. Hartman was supposed to file a 1983 civil rights racketeering action for me against Little Egg Harbor and Waretown. At around 2007, because he knew of my bankruptcy issue, Mr. Hartman recommended a forensic accounting firm to me – Gramkow, Carnevale, Seifert & Co., LLC. Representatives from this firm came to my house. I explained to them what was going on and that the firm of Heilring was trying to collect my assets, personal and corporate. Since most of the money in my bank account was in the corporation this was my main concern. Gramkow retrieved all of my financial records which was about 8 years of tax returns. They took every piece of paper I had which was an immense amount since I was building homes. There were many contracts and accounts for materials. They took a $5,000 retainer from me and they said that they would handle it. They started advising me what to do with my company and the money I had. They advised me to take the money out slowly and use it to pay my bills because they said until Heilring acted on the judgment it was still legal for me to do what I needed to do with this money. So, since they were experts in this field I listened to what they said. In fact, they told me to say that I went to Atlantic City and lost it. Can you believe that? Some time passed and, after my deposition with Heilring, the accounting firm was called in by Heilring to be deposed regarding my financial records. A day or two after the deposition I was contacted by this accounting firm and they informed me that they could no longer be my accountants as they had a conflict of interest. They told me that the Heilring firm was one of their biggest clients (can anyone believe this). Gramkow definitely had a clear conflict of interest which they never disclosed to me. It sure looks like I was being set up by Hartman.

Gramkow, Carnevale, Seifert & Co. then dropped me as a client. One of their representatives advised me that all of my files had been sent to another forensic accounting firm. However, when I ask to whom my files were sent I got no response. After several attempts at getting my files returned to me I was suddenly told that all of my files were lost in the mail and there is no record of where they were sent or who received them. My files were sent out without my permission. And there is no accounting of it. I have a taped conversation with one of Gramkow's representatives where he states that my file was LOST and he has been unable to track it down with the post office. He said it was in post office heaven. Not only were the banks screwing me around; but, now forensic accounting firms that were supposed to be the best in the business were too. I found it hard to believe that all of my files and records were suddenly lost without a trace. I found out later that basically what Gramkow was advising me to do was actually structuring. What their advise to me should have been, which I know now, is to leave the money in my corporate accounts. Heilring could not touch the corporate accounts unless he took over the corporation and, since the debt of the corporation was more than was in the bank accounts, they could not touch that money. Why didn't this high profile accounting firm know this. I am far from being an expert and at the time I did not understand that they could not touch the money in the corporation. A lot of this money was construction draws from banks for construction that I had going on. You see, Heilring needed that money out of there. They needed a way to get to me and that is why this accounting firm was recommended to me. Right from the beginning this accounting firm knew who they were going up against. They did not know the name of one of their biggest accounts? On top of everything else my entire retainer is gone and they did not one stitch of accounting for me and my files were never seen again. Again, I spend two years in federal prison and not a single person lost their job over this blunder.

**see: www.whyiwenttojail.com CHAPTER 9 - AUDIO 1 and DOCUMENT 1**

In addition, at this time Francis Hartman told me that he had to drop me as a client because he was not doing civil law anymore. After two and a half years he let my statutes of limitations run out for use of my tapes in a lawsuit and he dropped me as a client. He never disclosed to us that he was an ex-township attorney in Ocean County. We found that out much later. Apparently, he was brought into the picture to kill my lawsuit and set me up with this accounting firm. We found out later that he did this to someone else who was having the same problem – the Magliones whom we discussed earlier.

After the deposition with Heilring I provided Judge Lyons with evidence that my husband never had an account with Global despite the fact that Heilring must have produced documentation to the contrary. Thereafter, Lyons dismissed the suit against him. He also dismissed the criminal suit against me regarding Good Faith and changed his ruling for yet a third time. You have to understand these cases are filed for one reason. Heilring knew that these were phony allegations. They want you spending money. They want to bleed you and drain you of your finances so that when they give you the big hit you are unable to defend yourself. Lyons now awarded $243,000 from me to the trustee of Global Trading.

I am also denied my appeal for my case to go to trial and be heard before a jury. Judge Lyons had my appeal running in circles. My appeal never got to the right place. There was no way "they" were going to allow me to be heard before a jury of my peers. Summary Judgment means that there are no trials because the facts are very clear. The only people who saw the facts as clear were the judge and anyone else who wanted my land. And they needed me out of the picture. Summary Judgment should have been thrown out right away; but, "they" had Judge Lyons in their pocket and he flat out refused. I was kept running in circles spending money on legal fees – money I no longer had.

I received a letter dated July 29, 2008 from the US Department of Justice stating that Brian Winters and Global Trading owed me $215, 750. In one minute I'm being sued in Summary Judgment for my involvement with Global

Trading and later the US Department of Justice sends me a letter stating that I am actually owed money? Heilring had to know about this. He or a representative of his firm had to be present at the hearing regarding this. At this time I hire another attorney, Mike Pinsky, to represent me regarding my indictment. And as you are about to see, it seems to me that every lawyer knew that I was an easy mark to steal money from. When I say that everything was taken from me – I do mean everything. For whatever reason, Pinsky refuses to present this award letter to the judge. Pinsky's refusal would be yet another nail in my coffin.

**see: www.whyiwenttojail.com CHAPTER 9 - DOCUMENT 2**

Thanks to everything that Van Pelt and company were doing to me my construction company was at a halt. I had no other choice but to file for bankruptcy. I was shut down and I had no money left to launch an effective counter attack.

I hired attorney Jules Rossi to file my bankruptcy. Jules Rossi, my accountant, Anthony Mallozzi, and I documented where every cent I made was spent. Despite the very detailed accounting which took months to prepare, the trustee fought my bankruptcy proceeding. It was not long after this that the government filed structuring charges against me.

When Attorney Hartman bailed on me, the government now had a clear road ahead of them to begin filing the structuring charges against me.

Jules Rossi was one of the few attorneys that I hired that had my best interests at heart. He fought them tooth and nail for my family and I. He basically won every argument and referred to this as "the biggest witch hunt that he has ever seen". For such a small case the money they were spending was boggling. Finally, Rossi negotiated a deal for a settlement agreement between me and Global's trustee which was signed in April, 2009. The settlement agreement terms were as follows: I had to pay the trustee $110,000. Upon signing the settlement agreement I paid the trustee $40,000. I cashed in my SEP, my only retirement fund, to obtain this $40,000. One year later I had to pay an additional $10,000 and then $60,000 18 months thereafter. The $60,000 payment was collateralized by two of my husband's cars in case I defaulted on that payment.

I had no choice but to sign the settlement agreement with the trustee. I needed more time to make the second payment of $10,000. After several attempts by attorney Rossi and myself to request an extension, the trustee turned his back on us denying every request. The trustee then made the claim that we never made the cars assessable to him. This was clearly a false claim because the original titles to both autos were sent to him upon the signing of the agreement. To this day the titles show that they took ownership of the cars. This means my deal was complete. The trustee was actually paid in full according to the terms.

This is where my indictment begins.

While all of this is going on – and now Chris Christie's office is well involved – US Agents from the Federal Attorney's office came to my door asking to speak to me. They served me a notice stating that I had to contact the US attorney's office regarding illegal aliens. When we read the letter we initially thought it was a mistake – no big deal. This is when they put the hammer down. We were already fighting the townships, numerous law suits, the Heilring firm, allegations on my son, the IRS and now this - the final blow. This was now a full-court press. There wouldn't be anything that "they" weren't willing to do to make my torture as painful as possible moving forward.

"They" came after both of my children. I've already spoken about what they did to my son, making up lies about him bringing weapons to school to harm other students. Also, accusing my son of plotting to kill his girlfriend's parents in a school he did not even attend. I could not make up this nightmare if I wanted to. But then they crossed yet another line. They came after my daughter when she was very young. She's the younger of my two children. Friends and cohorts of Chris Christie don't care who they go after. It was just recently during Christie's presidential campaign that Christie bullied a little girl who quoted him correctly on what he had said about humans contributing to global warming by breathing. Christie ripped the microphone out of her hand and told her to "go home and clean out your ears." So going after a little girl is nothing new for these guys.

**see: www.whyiwenttojail.com CHAPTER 9 - VIDEO 1**

My daughter's school called my house and said that she was emailing pictures of people having sex with animals. Obviously the people that came after me were sick to come up with a plot like this to go against a young child.

Thankfully the Principal of her school did some investigating of her own and uncovered that the pictures were never sent from my daughter's computer – they were sent from a computer in Waretown. I can assure you that this was no coincidence. All of the troubles started with Township Officials from Waretown. No one but an animal goes after a little girl. Even the mob won't cross this line. Can you imagine being a mom and having your children exploited for no other reason then to discredit you. Not even an animal would stoop this low.

I was investigated from 2008 to 2010. US Assistant Attorney Joseph Gribko waited until the very last second to release my indictment. If he had waited any longer, even one more day, all of the statutes would have run out and their case would have gone up in smoke. And of course, waiting for the very last minute was just another ploy to make my torture as painful as possible.

My attorney at the time, Joseph Bondy, asked Gribko to give him a heads up as to if or when he was going to indict me. That heads up never came. Bondy also kept asking Gribko why was he so hell bent on coming after me for such a small amount of money, $200,000, especially when there was an agreement whereby the trustee would have been paid in full. Bondy asked repeatedly why "they" were so interested in putting me behind bars for an amount that really added up to chump change in the grand scheme of things.

They told Joseph Bondy and later my defense attorney, Mike Pinsky, that they really wanted my husband. If you think about it my husband was, for a time, the face of the company. It was he that kept rattling their cages. On all of the tapes Van Pelt and Von Scmidt can be heard saying how much they dislike my husband. Their investigation lasted two years and they found nothing on Robert. I believe that is why they went after me so hard. They were trying to get my husband to admit to something that he never did. This was all about them teaching us a lesson. How dare my husband and I collect so much evidence against them; how dare we make them look like the criminals they are. "They" were going to make this as brutal and as public as possible. All of New Jersey was going to see that this is what happens to people who get in the way of Chris Christie and his friends. Again, Christie had no problem reducing a little girl to a laughing stock in front of her friends, family and her entire community. All she did was quote him correctly – I had them all on tape acting like a pack of wolves moving in for the kill.

All of our attorneys were selling us out one by one around this time. All of my properties were being hit with new rounds of violations. "They" were coming after my family and, with the IRS auditing us, how could I even fight back with all of my financial records lost in the mail. I can track Christmas presents online that are being delivered to my house; but, no one can track where all of my financial records that were shipped out of one of the most prestigious forensic accounting firms on the planet went to? Give me a break – I wish somebody could have.

My indictment read that I committed bankruptcy fraud and structuring. It stated that I withheld $500,000 worth of guitars and $5.7 million worth of land in my bankruptcy proceeding. They brought this to the grand jury. They clearly knew that the guitars were my husbands and not mine. I do not even play the guitar. My husband has collected guitars since he was 13 years old when he first started playing. The land was only worth $5.7 million if it was subdivided and improved; but, since I was being blocked every step of the way, the land was not worth nearly this amount of money. Also, since they had Shore Community Bank with Howard Butensky and Joseph Mezzina leading the way they had people that were going to testify against me. That was their ace in the hole. In addition, since my husband had to give them all of his assets on the loan applications for the bank they were going to use those assets against me even though they were not mine. Soon it would be clear after they got what they wanted that the truth would come out of what the assets were REALLY worth and who was the legal owner of the guitars.

I could not afford New York Attorney Joseph Bondy any longer. We had nothing left. I could have sold the guitars but they were destroyed in a flood in my house which I will discuss later. I had to hire a defense attorney, Mike Pinsky, located in Haddonfield, New Jersey. Pinsky eventually talked me into taking a deal after his numerous meetings with US Attorney Gribko. When we first met Mike Pinsky he was pleasant and cordial. After meetings with Gribko, however, Pinsky became very hostile towards me. There was something that was just not right. My husband repeatedly told me to fire him. In fact, a friend, Barry Bendar, who I spoke about earlier in the book and was the Lacey, NJ democratic chair, called Pinsky on the phone. Barry would tell me that they got into an argument because it was obvious that Pinsky was not defending me. Barry told me that he told Pinsky "what side are you working for because it is obvious that it is not for Ms. Parise". I did not listen to either one of them and Pinksy talked me into taking a settlement plea. He told me that Shore Community Bank was going to testify against me and that the accounting firm that I hired was going to testify against me so there was no way I was going to win this case.

Pinsky told me that I would probably get 6 months house arrest. Even on the day of my sentencing with everyone there on my behalf, Pinsky stated that the Judge was going to go easy on me and go way below the guidelines. This was the farthest thing from the truth. Judge Wolfson added two points to my sentencing guidelines despite the fact that both attorney Pinsky and DA Gribko agreed that they believed that adding the two points would be double dipping.

The judge told both attorneys that they did not do their homework and, after doing her research, she believed the two points should be added although my family and friends begged for leniency. These two points added six months to my sentence. My family and I were devastated. Let's get back to my indictment.

In regard to the structuring charge, I already documented the accounting firm that advised me to do what I did and told me it was legal. Many people would read this and say that it was "BS"; but, I ask you how you can account for the fact that the law firm that was bringing these charges against me was one of their biggest clients. They never mentioned this as a clear conflict of interest. Not until they went to the deposition and gave evidence and conveniently lost all of my files in the mail. I have two of their accountants on tape telling me that they lost all of my files in the mail. So, this is not something that I am making up. I have hard evidence.

The third charge in my indictment was lying under oath at a deposition. This charge was dismissed. I plead to bankruptcy fraud which carried the least amount of prison time. When I went to my plea agreement I had no choice but to admit the value of the guitars and the land. There was nothing I could do. They had people that were going to testify against me. Prior to my sentencing many people had written character reference letters to the court on my behalf. On the day of sentencing some of them were there to speak to the judge. Something funny happened however. Mike Pinsky, my defense attorney, told all of my character references NOT to talk about the torture my family and I were going through and NOT to talk about the tapes because the Judge would get angry if those facts were brought up. Pinsky told them that this information was not pertinent. Once again, Barry Bendar and Pinsky had words with each other. Barry could not understand that this was my life and, since we had all of these people on tape stating how I was being tortured, that the Judge would not take any of this information into account. Pinsky clearly had his orders. Would you believe a Federal Judge would not take this into consideration and does not want to hear about federal corruption in New Jersey. Could the Judge have been part of this too? What she did not hear in court she would not have to address. So, make sure it does not come up.

The day of my sentencing Pinsky became the most incompetent attorney I had ever met. He told the court that my house was flooded because of Hurricane Sandy. I never told him that. Also, he said that I never tried to pay back any of the money. That is the farthest from the truth. I paid back $40,000 upon signing the settlement agreement. In addition, the settlement agreement enabled the trustee to take ownership of two cars that would have paid them in full. Nevertheless, Pinsky refused to mention this. It was like he didn't even know who I was. After this display the Judge was clearly angry at Pinsky for stating that the house was flooded because of Sandy. I had to stand up in the courtroom and correct him. The Judge stated that she did her own investigating on me, threw out my plea agreement and gave me 24 months in jail. The funny thing is – this sentence was already given out in the press hours before I was in front of the Judge. How do you explain that?

This was clearly an orchestrated plan by everyone involved; even my own attorney.

# 10. THE TRUTH COMES OUT

What they did not want anyone to know and what they hid...

It was discovered that in July, 2008 I was awarded by the Federal Court $215,750 in restitution with regard to the Global Trading matter. That means I owed them $27,250. Since I already paid them back $40,000, I over paid them $12,750. I find it very unlikely that US Attorney Gribko did not know about this order when it came out of his own court. Why was this information kept from me for years? Also, the Heilring firm, who represented the trustee, had to be present at this hearing when I was awarded this money. They conveniently forgot about this? Or, did they just have a game plan to follow? How is it possible that I am a debtor and a creditor in the same case? At my sentencing Judge Freda Wolfson stated that she did a thorough investigation on me. Her investigation was so good that she missed this order from her own court. It gets better yet – at my sentencing hearing Judge Wolfson claimed that I never made an attempt to pay anything back. My settlement agreement with the trustee was filed with her court. Also, Heilring claimed that I never gave them access to the cars that were collateral in the settlement agreement. If that was true, how did the firm take ownership of the titles. To this date, they never released ownership and never gave me credit for the $40,000 that I paid upon signing the agreement. This is a blatant attempt to keep my total restitution outstanding. By not reporting the payment, Heilring did not have to give it back to the people that they claimed they were fighting for. And, they claimed that I am the crook.

**see: www.whyiwenttojail.com CHAPTER 10 – DOCUMENT 1**

In addition, Gribko claimed that I held back $5.7 million in land and that Shore Community Bank was going to testify to the value of this property. They gave this evidence to Gribko in 2010, even though I had professional real estate appraisals prepared for my bankruptcy petition which showed the actual value of the land. Also in 2010, Shore Community Bank went to the Ocean County court and got a $1 million judgment against my husband for the same land claiming that the property had no value and that they needed to be made whole on their mortgages. The county judge granted the judgment. This was kept a secret for four years and they waited until the week after my sentencing to notify my husband. Is this yet another fact that Mr. Gribko did not know about? This would have surely cleared me of the bankruptcy fraud charge. However, since the bank was in on the scam, everyone was happy. Why would the bank wait four years to send notice that they had a judgment? Who's orders were they under? The next thing the bank did was claim that all of the principle was paid on all of the mortgages – apparently by me. If that was the case, how did the bank foreclose and how did they get a judgment against my husband? My attorney, Jules Rossi, has repeatedly asked the bank to disclose who has paid these mortgages and how come my husband's judgment has not been dismissed. However, he has received no response from anyone. When you are connected to Christie and Gilmore and are part of their goon squad, you get anything you want. When this was brought to the attention of US Attorney Gribko by attorney Joe Bondy, Gribko just sat there with a dumb look on his face and explained it away as creative accounting. As we will show you later, he is a disgrace to his office.

Gribko also claimed that I held back in my bankruptcy filing $500,000 worth of guitars. As we discussed earlier when I was asked on my loan applications with Shore Community Bank to include my husband, I included the guitars as his assets. Gribko, Heilring and Shore Community Bank twisted this and claimed that the guitars were mine and used this against me in my case. This gets even better. In 2011, I had a flood in my house which ruined many of my husband's guitars. In 2014, there was a settlement with the insurance company. Since, in my case, they always claimed that the guitars were mine, we offered the settlement money to Heilring to pay my restitution. Now – here is the big surprise. Heilring turned the money down and conceded to the court that the guitars were always my husband's guitars. Once again, as I mentioned earlier, Heilring turned away money. In addition, Heilring wrote a letter to the court stating that they never knew about the guitars and US Attorney Gribko agreed that he never knew about the guitars. Clearly the guitars are spelled out in my indictment, clearly they were mentioned in my plea agreement and, once again, they were mentioned by Judge Wolfson in my sentencing hearing. Now, US Attorney Gribko, who prepared all of these documents, does not recall the ownership of the guitars and claims he knew nothing about them. I would like to use what was said to the grand jury by Gribko against him; but, he fully well knew that the evidence he presented is sealed and they will not make it public. Because, if he never knew about the guitars and he knew about the judgment against my husband and that the land was never worth $5.7 million, he never had a claim against me for bankruptcy fraud. Concealing evidence is a serious federal offense. When your governor has a great interest in protecting his friends who are robbing the state blind, these people can get away with this behavior under the blessing of the US attorney's office. And this behavior continues to date.

As you can see from the following documents Gribko was well aware of the guitars and the worth of the land. His office prepared these documents which began with my indictment in 2009 up until the sentencing in 2013. As you can see, in the last document dated 2014 he states that he knows nothing about the guitars. I think what we see here is a clear case of "selective memory". These documents can be viewed in there entirety on the website.

**see: www.whyiwenttojail.com CHAPTER 10 – DOCUMENTS 2, 3,4,5,6**
**see: www.whyiwenttojail.com CHAPTER 17 – DOCUMENT 1**

Also, in 2015, to add insult to injury, Shore Community Bank showed their face again. They waited almost to the day I was released from prison to list the Little Egg Harbor property that they claimed was worth $5.7 million for only $299,000. In addition, almost over night, thanks to Mezzina and Butensky, the Little Egg Harbor property was rezoned back to one acre. They went out of their way to rezone this same property to five acres to block me from developing it when I purchased the property years earlier.

In fact, my attorney Joe Bondy, who I re-hired after Mike Pinsky, discovered that Pinsky was being prosecuted by the same court for $1.5 million in tax fraud - something Pinsky never told me about. Was he really incompetent or did they have him by the balls? So, earlier when I mentioned that Barry Bendar, the democratic chair in Lacey Township, called Pinsky and had an argument with him and asked him who was he working for - me or Gribko, I guess the answer should have been

Gribko. In fact, after my sentencing the evidence about the value of the property was given to Pinsky who just had a dumb look on his face and said "I have no idea what to do with this". This man forced me into a plea which, if he would have done just a little bit of research, he would have found out all of this information. Clearly, Pinsky was owned by them.

# CHAPTER 10 - DOCUMENT 2

9/2011     INDICTMENT

from the Parise Accounts described in Paragraph

7(A), herein. Rather, Defendant MARJORIE PARISE

claimed that she had used all of the purported

profits that she had received from Global Trading to

pay off her bills, most of which she claimed were

legal bills.

8.    On or about July 7, 2008, Defendant MARJORIE PARISE

filed for individual Chapter 7 bankruptcy protection. That case

was captioned In re: Marjorie Parise, Case No. 08-22743 (RTL)

(Bankr. D.N.J.) (Hereinafter the "Parise Bankruptcy Proceeding")

On her bankruptcy petition, Defendant MARJORIE PARISE failed to

report millions of dollars in real estate holdings plus hundreds

of thousands of personal assets. Specifically:

A.    In the Parise Bankruptcy Proceeding Petition, Defendant

MARJORIE PARISE claimed to have $2,605,000 of real

estate property, and $3,000 of personal property. She

claimed to have no cash in the bank, jewelry, boats,

machines, or other personal items. However, according

to financial statements Defendant MARJORIE PARISE

submitted to financial institutions in 2007, she

acknowledged that she had $5,778,000 in real estate

property, $1,600,000 in furniture, $500,000 in guitars,

an $85,000 boat, $75,000 of machines, and $500,000 in

cash.

7

1/28/2013     PLEA

fourteen additional bank accounts that you controlled, which held more than approximately $440,000 in or about August, 2006?

12. Did you conceal this information from the trustee knowingly and with the intent to defraud?

13. On or about July 7, 2008, did you file for individual Chapter 7 bankruptcy protection, in a case captioned In re: Marjorie Parise, Case No. 08-22743 (RTL) (Bankr. D.N.J.)

14. In your personal bankruptcy petition did you claim to have approximately $2.6 million in real estate holdings, when in documents you submitted to a bank at approximately the same time you described ownership in approximately $5.7 million in real estate holdings?

15. In your personal bankruptcy petition did you claim to have approximately $3,000 of personal property, when in documents you submitted to a bank at approximately the same time you described ownership in approximately $1,600,000 in furniture, $500,000 in guitars, an $85,000 boat, $75,000 of machines, and $500,000 in cash?

16. At or around the time that you filed your bankruptcy petition, did you act knowingly and with the intent to defraud when you made these false statements?

17. Are you pleading guilty to the charged offense because you are in fact guilty of this offense?

Had this case proceeded to trial, the United States would have been prepared to prove through witness testimony, documents, and other evidence, each element of the charged offense. The United States asserts that Defendant Marjorie Parise's responses to the questions above will provide a sufficient factual basis for the Court to accept his guilty plea to the charge set forth in the Information.

Respectfully submitted,

PAUL J. FISHMAN
United States Attorney

s/ R. Joseph Gribko

By: R. Joseph Gribko
Assistant U.S. Attorney

cc: M. W. Pinsky, Esq.

6

# CHAPTER 10 - DOCUMENT 4

1   million in real estate holdings, when in documents you

2   submitted to a bank at approximately the same time you

3   described ownership in approximately $5.7 million in

4   real estate holdings?

5        THE DEFENDANT: Yes.

6        THE COURT: In your personal bankruptcy

7   petition, did you claim to have approximately $3,000

8   of personal property, when in documents you submitted

9   to a bank at approximately the same time you described

10  ownership in approximately $1,600,000 in furniture,

11  $500,000 in guitars, an $85,000 boat, $75,000 of

12  machines, and $500,000 in cash?

13       THE DEFENDANT: Yes.

14       THE COURT: At or around the time that you

15  filed your bankruptcy petition, did you act knowingly

16  and with the intent to defraud when you made these

17  false statements?

18       THE DEFENDANT: Yes.

19       THE COURT: And are you pleading guilty to the

20  charged offenses because you are in fact guilty of

21  this offense?

22       THE DEFENDANT: Yes.

23       THE COURT: At this time, Mr. Gribko, I'm

24  going to ask you to please represent to the Court what

25  the government would be prepared to prove at trial if

12/17/2013 Sentencing

29

1  entities that she controlled, and the amount of course

2  in those accounts before the structuring, as I said,

3  was almost half a million dollars and at no time did

4  she disclose those other accounts.

5      In her own Chapter VII personal bankruptcy,

6  Ms. Parise, again, failed to identify substantial

7  assets, personal assets, claimed to have no cash in

8  the bank, no ownership of jewelry, both machines or

9  other personal items.  Yet, in 2007 in a statement she

10  submitted to a financial institution obviously to get

11  some sort of funding, she acknowledged substantial

12  real estate holdings, furniture in the amount of 1.6

13  million dollars, $500,000 in guitars, a boat, and

14  other items.

15      At the time she claimed that she received no

16  income in 2007 and that her income in 2006 was

17  $50,000, again, in a financial statement she submitted

18  to financial institutions.  She acknowledged income in

19  2006 of $271,000 and in 2007 of $271,000.  Whichever

20  was accurate, I don't know.  Whether she received that

21  income or whether she was simply seeking to at that

22  point defraud financial institutions is impossible for

23  me to determine on this record.  But the bottom line

24  is the lies continued day after day for purposes of

25  hiding her assets and keeping them from victims.

Hon. E. David Millard          -2-          July 23, 2014

we respectfully request that the Court adjourn the
pending motion and maintain the status quo by
directing that the settlement proceeds remain in
escrow with the Superior Court Clerk.

The history of the Trustee's involvement with the
Parises is long and tortured going back ten years.
It involved extensive litigation in the United
States Bankruptcy Court and investigation of the
Parises' financial affairs.  The litigation
resulted in entry of a judgment for monetary
damages against Marjorie Parise and an
adjudication of fraud.  The matter was thereafter
referred to the United States Attorney for
criminal prosecution.  In order to assist the
United States Attorney in his investigation of the
Parises, our firm turned over all of our files to
his office.  The files still remain in his
custody.

Mrs. Parise was indicted and subsequently entered
a guilty plea.  She was sentenced in January, 2014
by the Honorable Freda L. Wolfson, Judge of the
United States District Court.  The sentence
included an Order for restitution in the amount of
$353,404.91 to be turned over to the Bankruptcy
Trustee for distribution to creditors.

At no time during our investigation of the Parises
was the Trustee advised by either Marjorie or
Robert of the existence of the guitar collection.
Indeed, the Trustee was advised that all of the
Parises' assets were encumbered by mortgages and
liens, except for two vehicles which had nominal
value.

I have conferred with R. Joseph Gripko, Assistant
United States Attorney, who also was unaware of
the extent and value of the guitar collection.
Mr. Gripko supports the Trustee's request that the
Court maintain the status quo pending formal
application for turnover of the settlement funds.

# 11. JOSEPH BONDY

Joseph Bondy is an attorney in New York City that we were referred to in 2006. I went to Bondy to file a civil rights action and, as I stated earlier, he tried to get Henry Klingerman involved. I told you how that turned out. After much investigation Bondy wrote a draft of a complaint in which he called the goon squad a cabal. A cabal is an organization of people who conspire illegal activities together. Like I said earlier in the book, the evidence we had was so great that Bondy decided to take us to the FBI. That was the moment which probably sealed my fate making it imperative that they prosecute me. Bondy, of course, could not have had any idea how corrupt the cabal, as he put it, was. He could not anticipate that it went up to the US Attorney's office which he would soon find out. I did not hire Bondy to represent me in my defense. He wanted a very large retainer and I just did not have that kind of money left anymore. I was bled dry. Then again, that was their game plan. In this country do not expect to receive decent representation unless you have at least $100,000 to pay an attorney. And you better get an attorney that is out of state and not connected to the inner circle. He must be untouchable. Bondy was hired after I was sentenced to try to get me released on an Article 35 which is when an inmate hands over evidence of other peoples' wrongdoings to reduce their sentence.

Bondy clearly knew from our past interaction about all of the evidence we had. He approached US Attorney Joe Gribko to have a sit down to present our tapes and any other evidence, presuming that Gribko never heard about any of the corruption we were reporting. Bondy then went to do some research on Gribko before the meeting. He called my husband late one night and asked if he knew the name George Gilmore. Rob almost dropped the phone. Barry

Bendar and other people down here always thought George Gilmore was the person behind the torture of my family and I. But, I never met the man so I never assumed this was true. When Rob asked why Bondy brought up Gilmore. He told him that Gribko's wife, now x-wife, worked for George Gilmore. Now I knew for sure who was behind this. After some investigation by my husband, Barry Bendar and Bondy, they found that Gribko got his job because of the recommendation of Gilmore to Christie.

When Bondy set up the meeting he told Gribko about the evidence we had including evidence on Gilmore. First, Gribko never mentioned any ties to Gilmore. Gribko's wife had an on line resume clearly mentioning that she worked for Gilmore. After Bondy set up the meeting he called my husband up and said "funny thing, all of a sudden her resume was changed and she did not mention Gilmore any more". Also, Gribko sent out an invitation to Bondy on social media requesting Bondy's friendship. Bondy called me up laughing and saying that Gribko must think he was a high school student. Bondy said that he never dealt with anyone like this before. I explained to Bondy who Gilmore was and that I was very scared for my safety and the safety of my family. Bondy went through numerous articles on Gilmore searching for whatever he could with his connection to Christie. In fact, he found it very strange that Gribko did not bring it up and actually recuse himself from the case. Right before the meeting Bondy got a phone call from Gribko and Gribko explained that his x-wife worked for Gilmore; but, that it was not a conflict of interest because they were divorced. Gribko said that the only conflict he would have is if there was some crime we were bringing in that included his wife. Let's see here. His wife works for Gilmore, her checks go into their bank account and Gilmore is helping to support his family and you don't have a conflict of interest? And everyone we spoke to confirmed that Gilmore was very instrumental in Gribko's getting his job. But, let's say for argument sake that you can't prove that. Gribko still took Gilmore's money and put it in his bank account. If this is not a conflict, I don't know what is.

Bondy set up the first meeting with myself, my husband and Barry Bendar. When we got there Gribko had an investigator from the IRS present. Bondy looked at us and said "what is this all about?". His feeling was that this was not a meeting to hear evidence about anyone else. It was a meeting to get more evidence on me. We sat at the meeting and told Mr. Gribko about the tapes and the extortion of our money. We presented him with the cancelled checks and evidence that the money we paid the township had disappeared. He had no reaction to the tapes and we argued with him that this is straight up extortion. He actually agreed that it was; but, then went on to say that the $50,000 they extorted from me was not enough for the Feds to get involved. He went on to explain that if it was something like $200,000 per person they might be interested at that point. The US Attorney condones extortion up to $200,000 per person. We could not believe what we were hearing. We then talked about Howard Butensky and Joe Coronado and all of the faxes with Joe Coronado's name on it regarding my 28 acre lot subdivision and we presented him with the tape that Coronado knew nothing about the subdivision. Gribko had an explanation for this too. Even though these faxes were given as evidence in a lawsuit when we sued attorney Thomas Gannon and came directly from the township engineer's office, Gribko said "you can not prove that he actually signed the paperwork we presented". It became apparent that Gribko was going to explain everything we brought to his attention away. We also presented to him the judgment against my husband from Shore Community Bank which clearly shows that the property was never worth $5.7 million. He didn't even want to look at it. At this point Barry Bendar was clearly getting annoyed. My husband brought up my son's problem where they accused him of having weapons in his locker at school. There was supposed to be a federal investigation in this matter. But, someone stopped it. To all of our surprise, Gribko stated that "it was not his office that stopped the investigation". It made it very clear to us that Gribko knew exactly what was going on and that he was doing his part as he was instructed to. It is a sad day when you realize that the people who are put into positions to protect the citizens of the United States are only there to protect the corrupt politicians. I, like most citizens, believe that these people took an oath to uphold the law.

We also told Gribko about my husband's social security and with the craziness that went on there. We even asked him if he could assist in getting our records to get to the bottom of this. He said that he would look into it; but, his body language told us that he was just yes-ing us to death.

Our tape conversation with James Mackie, head of the Waretown MUA, was given to numerous law enforcement people we knew out of state. One friend gave it to his cousin who was an ex-assistant US attorney in New York. After listening to the tape he could not believe the arrogance of Mackie and thought that he was going down. We live in New Jersey; however, where there is no law. If you are within the inner circle of Chris Christie, you get protection.

As we walked out of the meeting we just looked at each other in disbelief.

Now Bondy wanted to take a different approach for the next meeting. It was clear that Gribko was not going to do anything with our tapes. Even though they prove extortion and the torture of citizens in this state, he was not going to do anything about it. Then again, these were friends of Chris Christie. We knew of numerous wetland violations in Ocean County. Bondy knew an investigator for the environmental protection agency in Washington by the name of Mr. Udell. As Bondy explained it to us, if you drop a piece of paper off of your boat, Udell would come after you. That is how serious Udell was about his job. There were homes being built on land that was designated wetlands throughout Ocean County. No one else could buy these properties and build; but, the connected people seemed to have no problem. Bondy's plan was to put these properties together and under Opra (Open Public Records Act) we would pull the records on these properties and hand them over to Mr. Udell so that he could do his investigation. We were pretty sure that there were no records, which turned out to be the case. He also wanted to bring in a special investigator of his choice from outside the area for political corruption. Bondy felt that inviting Gribko to be involved was a way to tie his hands from blocking an investigation.

We began with one house in particular. This was James Mackie's house, the head of the MUA in Waretown. He is the gentleman that you hear on tape extorting $30,000 from my company. His house sits in the middle of an estuary, all by itself surrounded by fresh water streams (check out Google Earth photo CHAPTER 1 – PICTURE 1). His is the only house there – all by itself. He has a very large house, a huge garage and a swimming pool - all built illegally. Bondy had us start here and do an Opra request to the town to see if any permits were filed with the DEP. To our surprise there were no permits found. We then went directly to the DEP and filed an Opra request. Once again, no permits or requests for permits were on file. We were not surprised.

We also investigated the Waretown Deputy Mayor Robert Kraft's building. Kraft was part time Mayor/Deputy Mayor and one of the heads of the MUA with James Mackie. Kraft was able to purchase a large parcel of land right on Route 9 North in Waretown. This land was always designated wetlands and all potential buyers were turned away from this property because it was unbuildable. Kraft is also the owner of Meticulous Landscaping. He needed a building for his trucks and his hired help to live. We did some research and found a permit filed to clear some wetlands and install utility lines to this property. The next thing you know, the entire property was cleared. In addition, a huge building complex went up in this spot consisting of numerous garages and apartments over these garages. We were also told that somehow these apartments were zoned as low-income housing. There were also numerous storefronts built on this property. Upon submitting an Opra request to the township for permits on this project, we got very little information back. Once again, we sent an Opra request to the DEP and once again they had no records of any permits to build this complex in wetlands. What we accidentally found out during our research is that $3 million was missing out of the MUA accounts. We also brought this to Gribko's attention and, once again, he explained it away as creative accounting. I think it was obvious that this complex was built with taxpayer's money.

In addition, we submitted Opra requests for information on about 20 properties that a gentleman was building in Waretown. His name was Robert Lange. Robert Lange was also a Waretown land use board member at one time. Lange had the authority to approve these kinds of developments. We Opra'd property after property that he owned and was building on and we received nothing back from the town. We Opra'd the DEP and they had nothing – again. Overall, in Ocean County, NJ we Opra requested approximately 50 properties that were designated wetlands by the federal government. All of these properties were improved by township officials and not one piece had any records of any permits from the Department of Environmental Protection (DEP). Some of these properties I tried to buy some time ago and was turned away. One property in particular I had a contract on for almost five years where we tried to get wetland permits to build. We finally dissolved this contract with the owner of the property who had passed away and Lange purchased the property. Almost over night he constructed a house.

Dan Van Pelt went to jail for taking bribes because he had connections to get wetlands restrictions overturned. Apparently, all of the connected people in Ocean County had the same connections. This was part of the scam. People own property that have some wetland issues or the powers to be claim that they have wetland issues. The towns stop them from doing anything with the land and then local politicians buy that land cheap and develop it themselves.

There was something else Bondy had us look into. Earlier I told you about Joseph Mezzina and a contract on a piece of property we had for $55,000 where the people refused to sell to us at the last minute. Then Joe Mezzina came in and purchased it for his company for $60,000 and then the county paid Mezzina $400,000 for it, to preserve it as open space. The following are more "sweet deals" like this – even better. Across the street from my house there are two large parcels. One piece was owned by a friend of George Gilmore's, a local dentist. The second piece was owned by some heavily connected people to the politicians in Ocean County. Recently a large sign went up on the property saying that this property was owned by Ocean County Natural Lands Trust, Ocean County Board of Chosen Freeholders and that the land was preserved by the citizens of Ocean County. Barry Bendar and my husband went to pull the records on these properties. The dentist who owned the first piece paid $100,000 for it. The County came in and gave him $1.95 million. The closing attorney was – George Gilmore. It must be nice to be friends with him. The second piece of property was purchased by three heavily connected gentlemen who paid $300,000 for it. They were given $1.75 million for that piece of land. When you search for these properties; however, the tax map shows them in different places than what they actually are which makes it very difficult for people to find the records. Barry Bendar and my husband researched multiple properties like this and every time the property did not show up in the tax records on the actual streets they were on. Obviously, very connected people are making a killing at taxpayers' expense.

Bondy researched the donation records to various political campaigns. What he found was very interesting. When George Gilmore donated everyone else followed suit. Even some of the attorneys I hired in the past to protect me donated. It became very clear that if you wanted to stay in business in Ocean County you "followed the leader".

What was also happening at this time is that apparently "they" were getting worried about the various Opra requests that Barry and my husband were filing. I guess Barry and my husband were digging too deep. My husband had texted Bondy one day that he was being followed by a black ford pick up truck for a few days. My husband thought that he was being paranoid and did not report it earlier. But, one day Bondy asked my husband and Bendar to video tape some wetland properties located in Forked River, NJ. When my husband went to cross Clearview Street a black ford pick up came out of nowhere, hung a U turn and gunned it straight towards him. Rob ran to get out of the driver's way but the truck jumped the curb and went on the grass to hit him. Luckily, my husband was able to jump out of its way to safety. Most of this incident is caught on video tape. Who was driving that truck? – John Downing – a good friend of George Gilmore. Yes, this is the same Downing that harassed the Magliones and was seen on their block the night that the lug nuts were taken off the wheels of their car. The people in the pick up actually got out of the car and started yelling at my husband and Barry Bendar saying that they did not like what they were doing. They did not like the fact that my husband and Barry were pulling records on their property and they said that the county prosecutor had previously investigated them at the request of the Maglione's and that they were cleared of any wetlands issues. They also claimed that they had the proper paper work from the DEP. Actually, the county prosecutor does not get involved in wetlands issues. When we requested their records from the DEP they showed that there were no records found for the development of this piece of property.

### see: www.whyiwenttojail.com CHAPTER 11 – VIDEO 1

The police have now turned up the heat. My daughter is being stopped almost daily. They are even citing my two dogs. I have two small shih tzus that never leave the house. But, I was getting violations on them. Also, the township code enforcement was dragging this into court and writing violations for properties that we owned in the past; but, were now taken over by Shore Community Bank in foreclosure. These were untouched wooded properties that, for some reason, were now being cited for dead trees in the middle of the woods. Bondy instructed my husband to meet with the code enforcement officer at the property and tape the conversation which my husband did. When he asked her to show him the violations she claimed that in the middle of the lot there was a dead tree and we have to keep the property clear. When it was pointed out to her that the bank now owned the property, she said that it did not make a difference. She said that she was also looking at another piece of property that we used to own and that property had the same problem. My husband tried to point out that on Robert Lange's properties there were violations of soil conservation. One of them was right across the street from our property. She said that she did not want to discuss these properties. My husband said "then why are you discussing my property". She said that some one filed a complaint and she was not at liberty to say who that was. My husband said that he was going to file a complaint on Lange's properties which she refused to take. It was obvious that they were playing a game because we were digging up information.

At this point Bondy felt that with all of the videos and Opra requests and the attempt to run my husband over we had enough evidence to bring a racketeering charge. He tried to set up a second meeting with Gribko. He told

Gribko of his plan to bring Mr. Udell and an outside investigator for corruption in on the meeting. However, Gribko insisted that he had his own person that was good as the outside investigator. Barry and my husband disagreed with Bondy for letting this happen. They felt Gribko was just going to call Tom Mahoney, good friend and appointment of Chris Christie and the same Mahoney who blew us all off after the FBI was called off. Bondy felt that Gribko would not do that since we knew the connection. But, sure enough, the morning of the meeting my husband, Barry Bendar and Rich Maglione were supposed to meet with Gribko at 10:00 am at his Trenton office. They were all waiting in the lobby for Joe Bondy to come in. Bondy walked in the door and said "I just got a phone call from Gribko. Gribko told Bondy that the investigator was Tom Mahoney; but, that he would not be attending the meeting". Bondy got the phone call at 9:55 am.

It was clear at this point that we were getting blown off. Remember this is the same Tom Mahoney that investigated Chris Christie in Bridgegate – what a joke. Christie recently said in an interview that he could have told everyone in 15 minutes what took the investigation 15 months to find out - that there was nothing that they could find on him. Sure he could, he had his best friends investigating him, Mahoney and McGuckin. Joe insisted we go up to the meeting with Gribko anyway. They gave Gribko all of the evidence of our Opra requests, everything on my husband's social security, the tape of Downing trying to run my husband over and the incident with the Magliones when the lug nuts were taken off their car. The Magliones even had a tape from the township building inspector stating that George Gilmore gave him the order to sick the police on them. Gribko could not care about any of it. He looked at the ceiling and was totally disinterested. At that point Rich Maglione started yelling at Gribko. We all left the meeting disgusted. Gribko knew the whole time that Mahoney was not going to show up at the meeting. On the way home Bondy was in the car with my husband and he could not believe how well done this was – that they had every one bought and paid for. In the next few days Bondy reached out to Mr. Udell who basically told him that he got a phone call and "was told to stay out of it".

Recently, I have been watching the presidential race on TV. Donald Trump was saying that all politicians could be paid to do anything. This is so true. In our investigation we found out that George Gilmore was one of the biggest fund raisers for Ronald Reagan. Of course, he took Chris Christie under his wing and Christie became one of the biggest fund raisers for George W. Bush.

So when a letter came into Bush's office nominating Christie for US Attorney, Bush didn't care about the man's character and probably did not care about his qualifications. Bush just saw that he was a huge fundraiser and saw the donations that he was getting and signed off on Christie's position. This is how the country is being taken over by these corrupt politicians. They buy their way in. In Bush's 2000 campaign Christie raised $350,000 to qualify as a "Bush Pioneer". Also, Christie's wife personally donated $29,000. Even though Christie had no experience in criminal law and he had never so much as filed a motion in federal court, he was awarded the position of Federal Attorney of NJ.

Shortly after the second meeting with Gribko it was apparent that Gribko went back to report what we were doing and the heat got turned up more.

# 12. GOON SQUAD

If you are targeted, Christie and Gilmore put you on their list to be harassed by police officers, township officials and judges. Earlier I spoke about Downing who tried to run over my husband. He has a long record of harassing people. But, he is not the only one. The police department is very involved with this. Here are some incidents that we have dealt with on a constant basis.

We had brake lines on our car cut, we had throttle body cables in my car taken off and we had the wire to the brake lights cut and, in this incident, they even left a knife in the car as a warning. It was obvious that they were harassing my daughter at this point as she could not even drive down the block without being pulled over. We live on a cul de sac so there is no real traffic. But, every time my daughter would pull out there would be a police officer waiting on Route 9 to harass her. She was pulled over no less than 15 times for brake lights being supposedly out. One night she was pulled over by three squad cars. Six officers surrounded her car. Can you imagine being a 19 year old girl surrounded by six cops because your brake light is out? They never ticketed her for a brake light however. They were sending a message.

One Sunday afternoon my husband took our dogs for a walk in a county park in Lacey which is usually empty, Enos Pond. He was in the back of the park with the dogs when he got a call on his cell phone by a Lacey police officer that he needed to come back to the car. How did they get his cell phone number? When he got back to the car he was met by the county sheriff and the police officer that called him. They questioned my husband as to who owned the car and why he was in the park. The officer told my husband that he should not be driving in his town. The sheriff just smiled, waved and drove away.

There was another instance on a Sunday evening. My husband just got home from visiting me in prison. He came home and my daughter took out the car. She didn't get a few miles up the road when she was pulled over by two squad cars. They told her that the registration was expired which was not true. They also told her that it was illegal to drive a car with handicapped plates which were my husband's plates. They told her that she needed to call her father to come and get her and she could not drive the car home and issued her a ticket for obstructing traffic. This was 10:30 at night on a Sunday. There was no one on the road. My husband got within 100 yards with his car and another squad car pulled up behind him and gave him the same ticket, obstructing traffic. They were using my daughter for bait. Within 15 minutes both of them were issued summonses; but, not for what they claim my daughter was pulled over for.

This harassment still goes on until this day. They pull my daughter over constantly claiming that she looks like me. Is my daughter being targeted? How do they know what I look like? Does the ocean county police drive around town with my picture in their cars? Can you imagine having to check your car every time you leave the house to make sure that there was nothing done to your car to cause an accident. This has become a ridiculous situation between the police and the code enforcement officials in these local towns. If you think this cannot be true here are some examples of what happened to others that were targeted in Ocean County.

As I am writing this chapter I received an email regarding a recent incident. App.com released an article – "Little Egg Harbor Democrats get Death Threats". Two people running for office in Little Egg Harbor, NJ (the town that is basically run by Joe Mezzina and Howard Butensky) became a target. They were running against the establishment. The woman in the article said that she received a sympathy card in the mail. The envelope read "do not open until after November 3, 2015", election night. One evening her running mate went outside his home and there was a strange gentleman standing outside his house. He approached him and the stranger said "nice house and nice car – it would be a shame if anything happened to them". A few days later the running mate's house was burnt down to the ground. Of course the Ocean County Prosecutor, who just happens to be the ex Little Egg Harbor township attorney that I had problems with, Joseph Coronado, said that there was no reason for an investigation and that he found no wrong doing.

**see: www.whyiwenttojail.com CHAPTER 12 – DOCUMENT 1**

Another incident occurred on February 8, 2012. The son of Barbara Wolfred, the Waretown, NJ building department secretary (the woman that put her fingers in a cross when talking to my private investigator about me), was shot and killed by a Waretown police officer. The police officer was the son of Gary Quinn, the right hand man of George Gilmore in Lacey Township and the mayor. Wolfred's son was shot once in the chest and was killed instantly. The story goes as such: the Waretown police stated they got a phone call from someone in Freehold stating that Wolfred was going to commit suicide. Quinn was sent to the scene. The police recording of the taped conversation never said anything about a suicide. Quinn claimed that Wolfred pulled a gun on him. One news article claimed that there were 12 officers at the scene searching for Wolfred's gun. I find it funny that Wolfred was killed instantly with one shot. You would think that the gun would be right by his side when he fell to the porch. However, the story would have you believe that Wolfred tossed his gun into the bushes right before he died. By the way, when the gun was found it was empty. There was no investigation regarding this. Barbara Wolfred did many dirty deeds with Waretown Mayor Van Pelt. It makes you wonder if this was a message. Officer Quinn now has a cushy job with a government agency in Ocean County. (Mayor Quinn also controlled Downing. If you recall, Downing was seen outside the Maglione's house the night before the lug nuts were taken off the wheels of her car. In a more recent article, George Gilmore nominated Mayor Gary Quinn to be a County Freeholder. Quinn is moving up the chain the same way that Van Pelt did in Waretown.)

**see: www.whyiwenttojail.com CHAPTER 12 – DOCUMENT 2**

Another example is a recent article in the Asbury Park Press. A Tuckerton police officer let his K9 dog attack a 57 year old Barnegat woman, Wendy Tucker. He claimed that he went to pull her over and that she did not stop. The woman was scared. She did not know who was chasing her as the officer was in an unmarked car. The officer chased her from Little Egg Harbor all the way to Barnegat where she turned herself over to Barnegat police. Two Barnegat officers hand cuffed her and arrested her. When she was in custody with the Barnegat officers the Tuckerton officer let his dog loose to attack her. Afterwards he falsified his police report. This is not the first situation with this officer and is an example of the individuals hired for police officers in the local townships. As of February 18, 2016, Ocean County Prosecutor, Joseph Coronato (sound familiar?), is appealing a judge's decision to release the video taken by the police officer's dash camera of the attack to cover up this officer's atrocity.

**see: www.whyiwenttojail.com CHAPTER 12 - DOCUMENT 3**
**see: www.whyiwenttojail.com CHAPTER 12 – DOCUMENT 4**

The last example I am going to provide to you is probably my favorite because it includes Stafford Township Detective Gordon Von Schmidt of Waretown. It shows the character of the types of people I was dealing with when Von Schmidt and Van Pelt were trying to steal my property in Waretown. The Stafford police, where Von Schmidt was a detective, arrested a Doctor. While the Doctor was handcuffed and thrown on the ground he was beaten unmercifully. None of these officers were ever prosecuted for this act. However, there was one officer, Lieutenant McMennamin, who, when the time came to appoint a new police chief in Stafford, was stepped over. McMennamin had tapes that he had recorded of a fellow police officer bragging how they were round house kicking this doctor when he was down on the ground. Apparently, they were laughing and thought it was funny. The pictures of the doctor in the Asbury Park Press were brutal. Later McMennamin wanted to become mayor of Stafford and the tapes were basically used as blackmail. In the real world McMennamin should have been arrested for obstruction of justice. He was a police officer who swore an oath to serve and protect. He held these tapes for himself. You would figure that all of these officers would have been arrested and charged after the tapes came out. One of these officers was Detective Gordon Von Schmidt. In Ocean County, NJ which is run by George Gilmore; however, no one was charged and McMennamin became mayor of Stafford Township.

**see: www.whyiwenttojail.com CHAPTER 12 – DOCUMENT 5**

I can give you more examples; however, this would go on and on. So, when I titled this chapter The Goon Squad, it is not something that I just made up. As the Maglione's and the Wojohowski's will also tell you this is real and we all lived it first hand. The ruthlessness to take citizens private land is unprecedented.

# 13. SOCIAL SECURITY

E arly in the book I referred to my husband's social security disability benefits. In the mid 1990's my husband had a series of three operations within four years. These injuries prohibited him from going back to his previous employment as an electrician with Local Union 3 in Manhattan. In 1997, he was awarded social security disability benefits (SSD) which basically paid him the difference between what he was able to make and what he was making as an electrician. My husband was allowed to work and receive an income up to a certain amount. This SSD benefit was to subsidize his income. Shortly after we notified the authorities about our recorded tapes, around 2008, he received notice that all of the Social Security Disability benefits paid to him since 1997 needed to be paid back immediately.

After receiving the notice, my husband and I went down to the SSD Office in Egg Harbor Township, NJ. Upon arriving early in the morning we met with an office clerk who proceeded to ask us all of the standard questions as to why we were there. She took one look at the notice and said, "this is odd, we would never go back this far to collect an over-payment. Take a number because you really need to speak to someone."

We were speaking to this woman for some time before taking a seat and waiting to be called. She looked up what information she could and told us that her records showed that my husband had recently been to their office and that he submitted a set of W2 forms that indicated that he was working for some company in the area. That was a lie. My husband filed for SSD benefits in New York City. There would be no reason for him to show up in Egg Harbor,

New Jersey and drop off any type of form. My husband wasn't even a resident of New Jersey in 1997 or when he first filed for that matter.

This lovely woman pulled our file. My husband and I took a number and we waited to be called. Eight hours later my husband and I were still waiting to be called. This woman saw us still sitting there and asked us why. We told her that we were never called to be seen. She then looked in her computer and saw that every time our turn came up that we were put back into the bottom of the list. She went into the back on our behalf to see what was up. She also told us that when she asked her superiors why this was happening she was told, "to mind her own business." She said that for some reason they will not see you. I asked that if we came back the next day would we be seen and she said "apparently not".

This is where it gets creepy. She told us to leave and meet her behind the building. She came out the back door and bluntly told us, "you need to get yourself an attorney. Someone is playing with your file and no one here is going to see you today, tomorrow or the any other day."

We met with attorney Joe Bondy who filed an appeal on my husband's behalf. Actually, Bondy filed three appeals; none of which were ever answered. To this day my husband and I have never been given an answer as to why they discontinued benefits or why they demanded a refund.

After this my husband and Barry Bendar went to see congressman John Adler to ask him to request his SS records. Adler too was unable to get them. Adler's office was told that no one ever responded to the SS office. This also is a lie. In addition, the appeals were submitted by Joe Bondy. Bondy was never contacted after numerous attempts. With everything else that was going on, because at this point I was indicted, we never heard from the SS office again.

There came a time in 2014 that my husband had to go on social services because of my incarceration. He had a requirement to file for social security benefits. He hired an attorney, Howard Kraft, to resolve this matter. My husband explained to Kraft the situation and Kraft informed him that the best way to do get answers was to complete a new application, get it approved and to set up a meeting with the social security office. After that, Kraft explained, if they still denied my husband, he would put in an application for a hearing before the judge to force them to show what evidence they had that my husband was working. My husband went on line and filled out the application and submitted it. The application was then deemed complete and he was given a meeting in the social security office on January 2, 2015.

My husband went to this meeting and met with a gentleman to go over his application. At this point my husband was taking no chances so he put his phone on record and recorded the entire meeting. It was quite obvious that the gentleman was very nervous. Even his supervisor kept coming over to ask if he was OK. What was that about? The man claimed that my husband had to pay all of this money back from 1997. My husband informed him that he would not until he saw the proof that they had that he was working. The man claimed that my husband's time ran out to see the proof because no one responded to them in 2008. Of course, this was not true. We had the paperwork from Bondy's appeals and the letters that Congressman John Adler sent to the SS office. Now the story has changed. The gentleman claimed that the inspector general did an investigation and that my husband owned two companies. It was no longer about W2 forms. They claimed that my husband owned K & R Custom Homes and another company by the name KBH Custom Homes which we never heard of. We actually did a search for KBH Custom Homes in New Jersey and nothing came up. They also claimed that my husband owned these companies since 1997. However, I started the corporation, K & R Custom Homes, after we moved to New Jersey and I was the sole owner and principle of the corporation. So, how did the inspector general have records from a company that did not even exist yet. And, according to New Jersey's corporate records, KBH Custom Homes never existed. The man also claimed that my husband had an income. He said that the inspector general told him that. The IRS has no record of it however. And even if he had an income, he was still eligible to receive SSD benefits.

My husband asked how he could get a copy of his SS records from the inspector general's office. The man said that we would need the name of the investigator in the inspector general's office that did the investigation and get the records from him. My husband asked "is the name of the inspector on the report you were given from the inspector general's office?" The man's answer was "yes". My husband than asked for the name of the investigator. The man said that he could get it; but, that he would have to go in the back for it. The gentleman left for about ten minutes. When he returned he told my husband that there was no name associated with his file. My husband asked again "how do I get my records then?" The answer was again that you need the name of the person that did the investigation. My husband replied that he just told him that there was no name associated with his file. "So how do I get the name?" This was clearly a who's on first, what's on second scenario – going around in circles and getting nowhere. Two days later my husband received a letter refusing his application because he owned K & R Custom Homes and KBH Custom Homes. Then another letter came in the mail claiming that my husband did not complete the application which we know is not true because we have confirmation of a completed application on line. That is how he had the meeting scheduled in Egg Harbor because he had a completed application. The letter also stated that he told this gentleman that he did not want to file an application for SSD. Thank goodness my husband recorded this meeting. Howard Kraft than filed a motion for a hearing before the judge which also went unanswered. Jules Rossi, the attorney that did my bankruptcy, also requested a hearing. His request went unanswered also.

This situation was brought to US Attorney Gribko during the meeting with Joe Bondy. Immediately after, more letters came in the mail requesting the money back. They also claimed that there was a possibility that they were going to send the file to the prosecutor's office for prosecution. Clearly Gribko had shared information and they turned up the heat. This should have been a simple case. If they had evidence that my husband owned these companies, they needed to present it. They were accusing him of fraud. But, they didn't want to do that because they did not have the evidence. They could not go before the judge because this whole scenario was a lie. They just want to stop the money from coming into my home and keep us going around in circles. Barry Bendar did an investigation on who is in control of that office and he was told that it was yet another friend of George Gilmore.

# 14. THE WARRANT

This is how they got the warrant for my arrest: As you've already learned, from the first conversation between my private investigator, Greg Steiz, and Van Pelt, the two of them talked about how the building inspectors were torturing me. Van Pelt talks about how the inspectors in the area worked for my company. That was partly true. Jim McBrian worked for me for a little over a year doing finish carpentry and other labor as needed on various projects my company was working on. Van Pelt approached Jim and hired him off one of my jobs. Van Pelt gave McBrian a nice cushy government position. Jim took the job which came with more money and a bit more power. Jim was promoted to Building Inspector. Jim just wasn't smart enough to realize he was being set up. He was going to be the fall guy – he just wasn't smart enough to see it coming.

It seemed like the very next day after quitting work on my projects that Jim McBrian was out at jobs he worked on for me and others serving as Building Inspector for the town. He started failing me on everything. I paid good money to Jim – I helped put food on his table – and now he's failing me all over the place. To prove my point that this man wasn't the sharpest tool in the shed – he was failing his own work. He was coming on to my job sites that he was once responsible for - most or all of the work - and now he was failing them. Is someone that stupid to admit in official documents that the work he performed couldn't pass his own inspection? Either that or Jim McBrian was working for Van Pelt long before he quit working for me and did shoddy work on purpose. Both are very much illegal.

Jim failing all of my inspections cost me more than I probably paid him over his year of service. Once you get in with "them", it becomes like getting a license to steal – actually its extortion.

Now when it came time to file a complaint about the Certificate of Occupancy on a house I built on Adriatic Drive in Waretown, Dan Van Pelt and Gordon Von Schmidt gave the complaint to Jim McBrian to fill out. In case anything was going to go wrong Van Pelt and Von Schmidt wanted to make sure they had a way out and that out was making sure that Jim McBrian's name was all over everything.

He was the patsy. McBrian filled out the complaint; but, he sent it to the wrong address. McBrian sent the complaint to some address in Waretown. Why not send it to my home? They had my address – McBrian, of course, did. For over a year Jim was picking up his paychecks at my house in Manahawkin. He certainly knew my address. Also, in a recorded conversation between my husband and Daniel Van Pelt, my husband clearly states where we live - they knew.

Since I never received the complaint, the police were sent to my house (Oh yeah, now they have the right address.). I had to call and get an attorney to stop the arrest while the police were waiting in my home. The complaint the police were delivering stated that for three years someone was living in the house on Adriatic Drive in Waretown without a Certificate of Occupancy – a CO. The buyers of this home were the ones who were supposed to get the CO because I couldn't. The property was sold to them with the stipulation that they had to obtain the CO. This is when Van Pelt and Von Schmidt start turning up the heat.

# 15. LAW SUITS

My construction business was being stalled and drained of money by frivolous lawsuits brought forth by customers who were persuaded by attorneys associated with Van Pelt and company.

One lawsuit brought against my company was by John Russo Jr., a Toms River attorney. John Russo, Jr. is former New Jersey State Senator Russo's son. Russo was representing the Sloans who approached me and wanted me to build them a small ranch on a piece of property my company owned in Waretown, NJ. They asked us if they could prepare the survey because they wanted the house in a specific location on the lot. They handed us a survey that showed where they wanted the house positioned on the lot. The Sloans waited until after the foundation was poured and then wanted me to move the foundation ten feet over. This was a ridiculous request and, of course, I refused. Unless the Sloans paid additional moneys, since the foundation was exactly where they wanted it according to their survey, would I move the foundation. At this point I should have realized that I was being set up. Apparently attorney John Russo, Jr. was working for the Sloans. He is a very connected person in the political machine in Ocean County. George Gilmore even had him appointed as a judge. This held up our business for months. After loosing that argument the Sloans made numerous claims during the building process. They claimed we installed the wrong counter tops even though they signed off on it. They claimed we installed the wrong cabinets even though they signed off on it. They claimed we installed the wrong carpeting even though they signed off on it. It was a never ending list of complaints. The Sloans insisted from the very beginning that they needed to get into this house quickly. However, it didn't seem that way. It came to a point that I offered them their money back and wanted them to walk away from the sale. I knew they were trouble and it would have been easy to sell the house to another buyer. But, this is not what they wanted. It was obvious after a certain amount of time that John Russo, Jr. wanted to run us around in circles and keep an ongoing lawsuit against my company which was draining my money.

I finally got to the point where I thought I addressed all of their concerns and we set up a closing. They had something else up their sleeve, however. The night before the closing some one slashed all of the screens on the windows. Russo put a stop to the closing. This was not a reason to stop a closing. I had the manufacturer ship new replacement screens directly to Russo's office, but, he claimed that they were not up to his standards. I found out that Russo was working for the Sloans for free. This was part of my torture. The only one loosing money here was my company. Finally, I closed on the house.

When the Sloans moved in they claimed that they were cleaning paint brushes in the sink and the sewer line backed up into the sink they were using. They had pictures of the back up and claimed that I did not hook up the house to the sewer in the street. Although it was clearly documented that the township building inspector approved the line and its hook up, the Sloans insisted that it did not exist. My subcontractor stated that he installed the necessary equipment and billed me for its installation and the township gave the house a permanent certificate of occupancy. The pictures taken by the Sloans showed no water in the tubs or toilets – only in the sink. This defies the laws of physics. The tubs would be the first to back up since they are the lowest point in the house. Then the toilets would back up and lastly the sinks, since they are the highest point in the house. These pictures were fabricated for the suit. In a deposition the township inspectors claimed that they made mistakes and, even though they signed off on the sewer line, they said that it was not installed.

Days before the trial Russo went into court and claimed that he had new evidence that he needed to present to the judge. The Sloans went as far as to get a neighbor of theirs, James Rickmers, to swear that he saw me and my family in Home Depot one day in late December and that my husband told him that we intentionally did not install the sewer line to the house. Rickmers described my children as proof that he saw us as being three and four years old, blond and blue eyed boys. My son was 11 at the time with brown hair and my daughter was 8. The problem with Rickmer's story is that on the supposed day he said he saw us at the Home Depot we were all in Staten Island, New York.

My father had passed away and we were staying in Staten Island for a few days to attend the services. After John Russo found this out he had Rickmers conveniently change his story. Rickmers claimed now that he made a mistake and that he saw us in Home Depot in July not December. However, he had already talked to our investigator, Bowen, which we have on tape. In addition, he gave the judge a receipt proving that he was in Home Depot on the day he previously mentioned in December.

Rickmers should have never been allowed to be a witness in the case in court because it was not new evidence, as we were now talking about July instead of December. Russo basically lied to the judge. But see, even the judges are in on it and it became perfectly obvious that my attorneys, Schzaferman & Lakind, were in on it too since they did not object to this. They were letting them get away with this nonsense.

After several years of litigation and costly attorney fees, the night before trial, the Sloans dropped the suit. I told my attorney to sue them for a frivolous action for attorney's fees, however, Schzaferman & Lakind refused my request to my disbelief. To this day, there has never been a permit pulled for the installation of the sewer line to the house other than my company's permit nor has there been an inspection scheduled.

Some time later the Sloans called my private investigator, Ross Bowen. Mr. Sloan told Bowen that, "he should not have gotten involved with Dan Van Pelt because after cooperating with Van Pelt he was looking to screw him". Apparently, Van Pelt was now trying to get the Sloans to condemn their own house. Peter Sloan knew that, if he did this, he would bring down the value of his house. Van Pelt was looking to protect everyone just in case an investigation was started.

Another lawsuit was regarding a renovation my company did for a couple in Little Egg Harbor, NJ, the Murphys. Sean Murphy had a boat repair business and did work for my husband on several occasions. The couple wanted to expand their small ranch located in Little Egg Harbor and they hired my company to do the renovation. From day one on the job the Murphys took pictures as though a lawsuit was imminent. They had pictures of the excavation of their property. The Murphy's hired Sean McCarthy, a Point Pleasant attorney who was a relation of theirs (so they claimed), to file a lawsuit against my company. Once again, free representation.

The Murphys not only sued my company; but, they sued my husband and me individually also. The suit against us was for breach of contract and fraud.

The Murphys claimed that my husband represented to them that he was the president of my company. No judge should have ever allowed this claim and should have dismissed it because they had no evidence of this fact. Once again, the corrupt judges of Ocean County had their marching orders "let this in". I met with the Murphys at my home office to discuss the renovation. Was my husband present? Yes, he lives there and he had known Sean Murphy for some time. However, I prepared the construction contract and I signed off on it as the company's representative.

Upon signing the contract the Murphys handed me a $20,000 check to start work immediately. What I did not know is that, when they left my home office that same day, the Murphys went directly to the bank and attempted to put a stop payment on the check. They knew that it would take some time before I found out that the check was no good. Why didn't they just say that they changed their mind and that they did not want to start the work? Another set up. From the first day of construction the couple had Sean McCarthy at their house taking pictures after our workers left the site for the day. Who does this? Why did they already have an attorney taking pictures when the work just started?

My subcontractors did the best they could to make the Murphys happy and to satisfy their needs. However, it came a point when they could not put up with Debra Murphy's complaints and her disrespect and nasty treatment any longer. They walked off the job without receiving any future payments. At this point a lawsuit was filed and this is when I discovered that the stop payment on the check was put on immediately when the Murphys left my house after signing the contract.

The attorney I hired to represent me was Shackleton and Hazeltine located on Long Beach Island. They were about to screw me too. What I did not know is that they were also township attorneys throughout Ocean County. After lengthy litigation and exorbitant attorney fees, the Murphys were brought to an arbitration which they lost. Discovery was over in the case and they had no proofs of anything. The arbitration lawyer basically called Mrs. Murphy a liar. He told her "you handed the woman a $20,000 check and immediately stopped payment on it and never said a word". This is where Shackleton and Hazeltine comes in and screws me. Without me knowing, they refused the arbitration award which I legally won. Then they allowed the Murphy's lawyer, Sean McCarthy, to go to court and request to reopen discovery and bring a consumer fraud claim against us. On the day of this motion Shackleton and Hazeltine was a no show in court. The judge stated that he should not allow this to happen; however, since there is no opposition to it, he assumed Shackelton and Hazeltine agreed and the judge reopened the case.

At this point we fired Shackelton and Hazeltine and hired Francis Hartmen to take over the case. We did not know; however, that Hartman was an ex township attorney in Ocean County also. The case went to trial and Hartman and McCarthy picked the jury. Astonishingly, we lost the case. How do you loose a case when someone hands you a $20,000 check to start work and immediately puts a stop payment on the check, never says a word to you about it and lets you continue to work on the renovation? She was clearly trying to defraud me. But you see, law does not mean much in Ocean County court. The Murphys won their case. And without one stitch of evidence they won against my husband on the Murphys say so that he said that he was the president of my company. The best part was that they never presented any damages because of this. This should have been thrown out by any credible judge. Not in Ocean County though. Not when the judges are appointed by Chris Christie and George Gilmore. You do what they say. When the trial was over, we were leaving the court and some of the jurors were saying goodbye to Sean McCarthy, the Murphys attorney. I looked at Hartman and said "what is going on here?". He told me that McCarthy was a local politician and that these people apparently work for the township and that they knew him. Where was Hartman when they were choosing the jury?

A third suit was brought against my company by a Dr. John Adams. Adams hired me to build a second story on his bay front home located in Manahawkin. Adams handed me blue prints prepared by a local architect. I followed the architect's specifications during construction. Adams, like the Sloans and Murphys, started making frivolous complaints. One complaint was that he wanted me to preserve his 30 year old wallpaper on the first floor. This was ridiculous. I had to tear off the ceiling. How could this be done? There was another complaint regarding a heating and air conditioning vent. He did not like where the vent was placed, and any location that I gave him to put the vent he disagreed with. So, I asked him "where would you like it?". He would not tell me. His answer was "you are the expert". The funny thing is that my investigator had me tape Dr. Adams right before he made his first payment and everything was fine. But, as soon as he had to make the first payment, he had a problem. He did not like where the air conditioning vent was and refused to tell us where he wanted it. Of course, once again, Adams had a very connected local Toms River attorney, Kevin Riordan, and yes he was a friend of his that worked for free. "Do you see any pattern here"? I could not afford to fight another lawsuit. I walked away without getting paid. Shortly afterwards we discovered that Adams was friends with James McBrien, the building inspector in Waretown where Dan Van Pelt was mayor. McBrien originally built Adams' home. In addition, Adams' nephew was a builder in the area so why was he coming to me to do his renovation and not his nephew?

It became clear at this point that these lawsuits were brought against me for one reason and one reason only – to inflict the torture that Van Pelt spoke about on the tapes against me. Everyone played their part and did not step out of line. If you want to stay relevant in the corrupt Ocean County political system you do what you are told and kiss the ring.

# 16. ATTORNEYS

Over the course of my journey to prison, I paid many attorneys lots of money to represent my company and I. They all sold me out. Most were afraid of what would happen to them. It was easier for them to sell me out. That's how this state is run - by fear. To give you an example, Alec Macgillis, a writer for the New Republic wrote an Article called "Chris Christie's Entire Career Reeks". It was written on February 12, 2014. Barbara Buono, the Democrat that ran against Christie for his second term, made a statement that she could not get enough money to run a credible campaign. No donor would give above the $300 threshold where their names would have to be disclosed. They were all afraid of Christie's retribution. You could say that he was fixing an election by intimidation. I was having the same problem with my attorneys. Most of the attorneys I hired committed legal malpractice, better that then go against Christie & Gilmore. One attorney in particular, Keith McKenna, was a no show in court on many of my cases causing me to lose case after case. As a client they don't inform you when court hearings are scheduled. Only your lawyer knows. So, when he doesn't show up for court, you don't find out until much later when the damage is done. Case after case he let the other side win because he didn't show up in court, burying us in judgments. But, this was his plan. The one case he did fight, he took a $4 million case and turned it into $125,000. Then he had the check made out to him and took all the money. This was the case against Fox Rothschild for malpractice for blowing our multi million dollar subdivision. This case lasted over four years which is a ridiculous amount of time for a law suit like this. Even though I paid for five experts he missed the scheduling deadlines to produce this evidence. We had a settlement hearing in the court which McKenna, for some reason, wanted a second mediation in the case. I refused. I knew what he was doing. We already had one mediation. There was no need for a second. However, he had a plan to try to get himself out of trouble. He told us that the judge wanted us to meet him in the courtroom and he brought us to an empty courtroom. McKenna made believe that he was going to find out what happened. When he returned he had a piece of paper saying that we had a second mediation. What he did was fill out a request to the judge that both sides wanted a second mediation and put it in front of the judge for him to sign. Even though I insisted that this was something that I did not want, he went against my wishes.

Now he played a bigger game. He told us that we had to pick a mediator and this is when we realized that Fox Rothschild was in collusion with McKenna. He gave us four retired judges to pick from. For now lets call them 1, 2, 3 and Judge Camp. We did not know any of them. So we picked 1 and 2. But, of course, they were no good. He claimed that Fox Rothschild had a problem with them. Then we picked judge number 3. There was an issue with that judge too. That left us with Judge Camp. We went to the mediation and we believed that we had a judge who thought he was trying to get the case settled on our behalf. However, this is so far from the truth. Judge Camp was a long time family friend of Keith McKenna. What he was there to do was try to solicit answers from us to try to get Keith McKenna off the hook for malpractice for blowing this case. Here was a judge conspiring with a lawyer friend of his to defraud a client. And, this is not the first time they did it. In another case that I found out, McKenna and another judge swore in papers in another lawsuit that they did not know each other, but they got caught. Of course, in New Jersey, when you are connected all you do is get a slap on the wrist. Only people like me go to jail.

## LoMurro, Davison, Eastman and Munez

This is another law firm that I hired to file a civil rights suit on my behalf. They were also supposed to review my case for legal malpractice against attorney Thomas Gannon. This firm was very enthusiastic to take the civil rights case. Even Munez himself came down from his Freehold office to walk my properties in Ocean County. What I did not know was that I was being set up by this firm also. The lawyer assigned to my case was James Paone. He claimed that he had two drafts of a federal 1983 action which is a civil rights racketeering suit. But, he claimed that first I had to be brought to the Ocean County Construction

Board of Appeals. This did not make any sense. Actually, Paone was just trying to bleed me of my money. He brought me to the board of appeals twice. Of course, the attorney on the other side was none other then Gregory McGuckin, Chris Christie's best friend. Paone postponed the board hearing for months at a time holding up my construction projects. Finally, we received a date to appear in Toms River with my engineer who would testify on my behalf. Paone had a conversation with McGuckin outside the court room and then approached my husband and my engineer and refused to go into the hearing. My husband and my engineer were furious at this point. We just wasted a lot of money and now Paone didn't want to go into the hearing. He argued that he had assurances from McGuckin that our project that was being held up would be taken care of the next morning and that we would be able to proceed. He also said that he had enough on the record to proceed with his civil rights suit. The next morning I went to the job site to see if I was cleared to proceed. But, I had the same situation. When I went to the township to find out what was going on, McGuckin, with a big grin on his face, said that nothing was cleared and that we had no deal. He was laughing that my attorney should have gotten this in writing. Also, regarding their investigation into Tom Gannon and the potential malpractice, Paone claimed that I never had a claim against Gannon. Understandably, with the previous circumstances I walked away from this law firm. What I found out since is that LoMurro, Davison, and Eastman were co council board attorneys in Tinton Falls, NJ where Gannon was the planning board attorney. This is a clear conflict of interest. They were just trying to protect their friend. As I mentioned earlier, I sued Gannon using attorney Glenn Bergenfield and we won our case. In addition, what we found out is that LoMurro, Davison, Eastman and Munez were the Waretown bonding attorneys. You could not have gotten any more conflict of interest. This was straight collusion with McGuckin to run me around in circles. They were never going to file a lawsuit on my behalf. Also, Robert Kraft, who is the sometimes mayor and deputy mayor and one of the heads of the MUA in Waretown, would have had to be named in the civil rights suit. What we found out is that Robert Kraft's father is Jack Kraft. One of the main partners in the LoMurro firm is a Jack Kraft who just so happens to live in Waretown.

Some time later my husband was having trouble with his cell phone. The battery was getting hot and the phone was running down. He brought it back to the store and they told him that there was spyware in his phone and that it was continually running because someone was tracking the device. He had to change out his phone numerous times because of this. I mentioned this because what happens next is scary. Over the past few years we were meeting with numerous attorneys to file malpractice or civil rights cases. Many of these attorneys were enthusiastic since the cases were blatant. But, after several days these same attorneys would not return our calls or they would tell us that they were not interested any more. We felt some one was getting in touch with them and steering them away from us. But, I had no proof of this. So, in 2014 when I was incarcerated my husband approached my bankruptcy attorney, Jules Rossi, to file some of these cases. Jules was about the only attorney that we could trust. However, Jules had medical issues. This is why we did not approach him sooner. He agreed to take on the case with the help of a friend of his, attorney Bill Gallagher. My husband had a preliminary meeting with Jules and Gallagher in his office just to talk about how to proceed with the cases. Gallagher was very enthusiastic about these cases in the meeting. What happened next confirmed my fears. Jules Rossi contacted my husband and told him that Gallagher was no longer interested in taking on the cases. Jules told me that Jim Paone contacted Gallagher and told him that he was one of the original attorneys on the case and that all of our tapes and evidence were fraudulent and that it was in his best interest to stay away from us. But, how did Paone know about Gallagher? Gallagher did not file any paperwork with the court where Paone could have seen it. This was just a preliminary meeting. It became perfectly obvious that someone was listening to our phone conversations. And if Paone did this to Gallagher, he did it with everyone else.

Finally, Giovanni DePierro was an attorney recommended to us to look at a case against Keith McKenna for intentionally screwing up all of our cases. I mentioned to you in the beginning of this chapter that they had a way of dealing with all of these potential legal malpractice suits. DePierro was their fix. He asked us for all of our files. He wanted everything. We gave him approximately 8 boxes of files which, to this day, he refuses to return to us. DePierro claimed that he was going to review the files and bring a legal malpractice case against McKenna. DePierro, without our knowledge, filed malpractice claims against every attorney that he could find in our files that could have potentially committed malpractice on my cases. Then DePierro got all of his filed cases dismissed with prejudice so that I could never bring a case against any of these attorneys. He took them all off the hook for malpractice. This is why so many attorneys were committing malpractice without thinking twice – they knew that they were being protected. DePierro could not do this on his own though. He had help from a long time friend of George Gilmore, Judge Mallard. Mallard dismissed approximately 15 cases with prejudice blocking every law suit from ever being brought again. He also dismissed with prejudice a personal injury case that we had with some very questionable rulings. Over the years any case that was filed on my behalf always found its way to Judge Mallard's desk. This was no accident. He apparently had his orders from Gilmore. They wanted to make sure that I would not collect any damages on any case to keep me broke.

## Anthony Malanga

Anthony Malanga was an attorney that I hired to clean up the mess that Keith McKenna made of the lawsuits I had hired him to handle. The first of these was to finalize a lawsuit against Daniel Van Pelt and Robert Kraft, the mayor and deputy mayor of Waretown. A short time after that lawsuit was completed, we were in a car accident and then had a flood in our house due to a washing machine failure. All that Malanga had to do in regard to the car accident case was to file a no fault claim so that my husband could receive medical treatment. My husband was hurt badly in the accident. Even though I received numerous emails from Malanga stating that he filed the no fault and was waiting for dates to go before the judge, it never came about. With regard to the flood in my house, the insurance company was refusing to pay for the damages and lost possessions. There was over $700,000 worth of damage. When the insurance company finally repaired the house their contractors left wet insulation and duct work in the walls and closed the walls up. This caused the house to become toxic with mold. Both my daughter and husband became very ill with mold poisoning which led to them having asthma. My husband had to be hospitalized many times for his condition. My daughter who was a singer in a performing arts high school had to be home schooled for two years and had to eventually give up singing because of her condition and still suffers serious health issues today. Malanga filed three suits in regard to the flood. One was for the damage to the house and its contents, the second was a personal injury case for my husband and daughter and the third case was for errors and omissions against the broker. Malanga never bothered to do discovery, he never did a deposition, never talked to any doctors or ordered expert reports. Did he somehow know something we didn't know? Finally, my husband was brought into court to pick a jury for the damage case against the insurance company. He was totally unaware that the other two cases were dismissed because Malanga had never pursued them. Malanga tried to convince my husband to settle the damage claim that was worth over $700,000 for $165,000. My husband repeatedly said no that he did not want to settle. In fact, he was brought before the judge and he told the judge that he did not want to settle the case. After leaving the courtroom my husband was told to go home and that it would be rescheduled for another day. What Malanga did next is outrageous. He went back into the courtroom and settled the case. And, the judge accepted the settlement without hearing from my husband and without any documentation stating that my husband wanted to settle. Why would a judge do this? He just heard from my husband that he did not want to settle just minutes before. The judge was none other than George Gilmore's friend, Judge Mallard. In fact, Mallard went as far as to dismiss all of the other cases and claimed that my husband knew that the personal injury case was part of the settlement. He also said that Malanga was asked if there were any other cases pending and Malanga told him "NO" which was a flat out lie. We recently found out that attorney Malanga is up for disbarment. We understand that the charges against him are that he was stealing clients' money out of his escrow accounts and forging court documents for his clients. Just like my defense attorney, Mike Pinsky, they had him by the short hairs, and he was going to do anything that he was told to do. As a side note, we did not receive a single dime of the settlement funds.

**see: www.whyiwenttojail.com CHAPTER 16 – AUDIO 1**

# 17. CLOSING

People have asked me why I am writing this book. They feel that I should just move out of New Jersey and go on with my life. The public needs to be warned that, today it was me that was sent to jail, but tomorrow, it could be any one of them who like me, refuses to give in to the "machine". People need to be made aware of what is really going on just outside their front door. Just like me, the Magliones, the Wojohowskis and the Horners found out the hard way just how corrupt local government in Ocean County, New Jersey is. There were many other people I wanted to include in this story, but they were too afraid of retribution and asked me not to. I've also often been asked why I didn't go to the press with this story. They do not understand, as I certainly do now through this experience, that the press is bought and paid for. They write what they are told to write by those in power. As an example, NPR (National Public Radio) was running many stories regarding the antics of Governor Chris Christie. One reporter, Matt Katz, authored many of them. When he was running stories in regard to the "Bridgegate" affair, he was contacted by Barry Bendar, who brought to his attention that some of those investigating the scandal were close friends of Chris Christie. One was Gregory McGuckin who was on the state assembly investigating committee. The other was Tom Mahoney, the investigator in the Federal Prosecutors office who was a "leftover" from Christie's regime in that office. To our surprise Katz insisted that there was no connection. He was presented with many internet articles which document that these connections are true. Eventually he admitted that there was a connection; but, he felt it wasn't that important to the story and he wasn't going to report on it. On my way to incarceration it would have been nice if I had my friends investigating me! The bigger question is, why would such a liberal news organization be willing to let Christie "off the hook"? Matt Katz had a book coming out; however, I guess the truth did not fit his agenda. There was also stories printed in local news papers of how I sued Waretown. Christie's friend, McGuckin, gave these stories to the press to print. Not one reporter checked if they were true. The only people who knew about the lawsuits were McGuckin and the press. Not even the court heard about them. They just printed what they were told to print to help the lie. In a town meeting McGuckin even claimed to win one of these lawsuits for Waretown. He said that they won the missing $50k they extorted from me in that suit and that they did not have to account for it. When Trump says in his speeches that the press is garbage, it is so true. They are as corrupt as anyone can get.

Another example was more local. In the summer of 2012, we began working with a reporter named Colleen Platt from the Barnegat/Waretown Patch, a local online news service, on acquiring more information on the whereabouts of the $50,000 we had paid to Waretown for road improvements and the waterline that we referred to earlier in this book. Via OPRA requests, we found that the road actually cost only $3,200 to pave, while the water line for the entire block cost $10,000, of which my portion would have been approximately $2,000. The reporter was going to help us find out what had become of the remainder of this money we had paid. At the October 11, 2012 Town Council Meeting in Waretown, Barry Bendar came forward and asked the council about the present disposition of the money. Colleen Platt, the Patch reporter, was in attendance. The Township Attorney, Gregory McGuckin replied to Mr. Bendar that the money "was a gift to the town" on my part, and would not be returned.

After this meeting, Colleen went to the new Township Administrator, David Breeden, with the evidence we gave her of our water line payment. Breeden told her he needed more time to research the payment. As 2012 rolled into 2013, and Breeden had yet to reply to the reporter's inquiry, we forwarded her the recording of James Mackie, extorting $30,000 from us, hoping this would give her incentive to push Breeden. After Colleen reported back to Barry Bendar that she was scheduled to meet with Attorney McGuckin to discuss the matter she no longer would return his calls. In desperation, Mr. Bendar contacted her boss at the Patch, Tom Davis. He was told by Mr. Davis that the Patch no longer covered Waretown, and if they ever did again they would re-address our story. So much for a "free press". However, the Patch was very quick to pick up the story of my indictment. Wouldn't it be nice to know what went on in the conversation between reporter Colleen Platt and Township Attorney Greg McGuckin?

Politicians bank on the public being ignorant. They realize that most people go to work in the morning, come home at night, and know little else of what goes on around them. They read stories in the newspaper and take everything that's written as "gospel". People very rarely analyze what they are reading. For example, in the Jamila Davis story, the press would have you believe that this young girl was the master mind of the Lehman Brothers financial failure. She was virtually a nobody in this company. Christie, in his role as Federal Prosecutor, needed someone to be the "scape goat" however. Of course, he was not going to go after his buddies that made an enormous windfall profit on the deals. Who better to prosecute this young woman and give her a sentence that most murders don't get. He expected the public to read this and say "Oh my god, she must have done something really awful to get such a long sentence". Then Christie got to pound his chest about his war against corruption. In the mean time, one of his Lehman Brother "buddies" (inside investor, Chris Lipka) acquired the properties in question for a fraction of their appraised value, and Davis was charged for the difference.

As a matter of fact, Davis had been subject to harassment by FBI Agent Sean McCarthy (yes the same Sean McCarthy who Christie brought in to shut down our investigation in the Red Bank FBI Office) beginning in May of 2003 as documented in a civil action (Civil Action No. 12-429 (JLL)) taken by her in 2013. She charged McCarthy and his cohorts with false arrest and withholding evidence. Sound familiar? Maybe the entire affair that caused Jamila to end up in Federal Prison was a set up from the start? Based on what I experienced, I wouldn't put it past Christie to create such a scenario to keep his "buddy" Sean McCarthy happy.

In my story, which spread like wildfire in the press, they would have you believing that I had over $6 million in my pocket, but I could not pay back $243,000 to the Trustee. Does that make any sense at all? If I had property worth $6 million, why didn't the Judge just confiscate the property, have it sold, and take the $243,000 from that? Not a single person who read the story, nor anyone in the press who circulated it as gospel truth ever asked that question. In her own statements at my sentencing, the Judge stressed that my severe sentence was because I was taking money from the seniors and young families who were the victims of Global Trading. As mentioned earlier, the bank had a judgment for $1 million against my husband they claim they were owed for the mortgages. If the properties were sold for the $6 Million they were supposedly worth, and the $243,000 for the Trustee and $1 million for the bank were paid out, that would have left me with $4.8 million. Is it possible the judge herself knew that the evidence was fraudulent and she could not make that order? Could she have known that the property was never worth $6 Million in its undeveloped state? How else could you explain her not attempting to get the people's money back and at the same time, covering for Christie's friends at Shore Community Bank who were making windfall profits in the deal. Why didn't the press pick up on that?

**see: www.whyiwenttojail.com CHAPTER 17 - DOCUMENT 1**

In the Bridgegate story, the press would have you believe that the bridge was shut down simply because the mayor of Fort Lee had not endorsed Christie in his re-election bid. Supposedly, the entire thing was planned out by a woman, Bridget Kelly, without Christie's knowledge. If you take a step back, and ask the question, "how did shutting down the bridge hurt the mayor of Fort Lee?" Wasn't this an extreme measure? The traffic this caused was a temporary problem for the Mayor and his town. As in my case, what this really was about was land. Just like Van Pelt was doing to me, Christie wanted to devalue a piece of property in Fort Lee that was very important to Mayor Sokolich. At the base of the bridge there was a redevelopment project that was worth a billion dollars to the town, per a story published in January of 2014 by Steve Kornacki of MSNBC. In the story it is reported that the 16 acre property had sat vacant for four decades, and was some of the most valuable real estate in New Jersey, thanks to its proximity to the George Washington Bridge, which serves as a gateway to New York City - and especially because it abuts the very local access lanes that were closed by members of Christie's team. By creating the traffic jam that the lane closings caused, Christie was putting this entire project in jeopardy. As a matter of fact, as reported further in Kornacki's story, the mayor, on that sorry day in September of 2013, wrote an email to Christie's point man at the Port Authority, Bill Baroni, asking "What do I do when our billion dollar redevelopment is put on line at the end of next year?" It was also pointed out in the story "that financing had not yet been finalized for the redevelopment of the second half of the land", "and it was those access lanes that made the land particularly valuable, both to developers and potential tenants". The Bergen Record reported on September 16th of that year that financing had - after an

134

unexpected delay - been finalized for the Hudson Lights portion of the redevelopment. That date - September 16 - came three days after New York officials at the Port Authority intervened to put an end to the lane closures. They would have us believe that the Governor that micromanages everything had no idea that this was going on. Someone had to take the blame. Who better to take the fall but a woman, Bridget Kelly. Kelly is probably going through the hell that I went through; but, I don't feel sorry for her. While she was under the protection of Christie she understood how this man operates and she would have never thought that when he got in trouble she would become the "scape goat". Funny thing is, that for never knowing about the plan, both Christie and Baroni gave comments in a December press conference and before the State Assembly Investigation Committee after the fact suggesting that the administration may have been looking to permanently close or reduce the number of access lanes that September. Was it retribution, or was someone not getting their "piece of the pie" on a billion dollar real estate deal? That's for you to decide. I just find it strange that this part of the story was never picked up by the mainstream media. Just remember the purported conversations between the Mayor of Hoboken and the Lt. Governor about that piece of property in Hoboken, NJ, owned by the Rockefeller Group. This is when the Lt. Governor supposedly threatened the Mayor of Hoboken that, if she did not go along with this project being promoted by these close Christie associates, that Hoboken would not receive a penny of Super Storm Sandy aid. And others involved in this little scheme were also some of the fabulous minds that brought you Bridgegate. See a pattern here?

The final warning of this book is, if Political Bosses with criminal intent control all levels of law enforcement including the courts and judges, what chance do you and I have, if we "get in the way"?

In closing, in the 50 plus years I've been on this planet, I have never been in trouble with the law in any way, shape, or form. It wasn't until I went to the FBI office in Red Bank, NJ with evidence of the extortion and racketeering that was being perpetrated against me by crooked Ocean County Politicians protected by Chris Christie, that suddenly I was a criminal mastermind and was immediately indicted. Funny this should happen right after we signed documents with the Federal Prosecutors office protecting us against just such a situation. No law enforcement authority wanted to listen to my recorded tapes or any of the other evidence that I had collected once Christie stopped the investigation in Red Bank. It was overnight that I was made out to be a hardened criminal. I never thought in a million years that I would go to prison.

It was twenty-four months that I spent in prison for a crime that I did not commit. There is no worse punishment for a loving mother and wife than to be taken away from her family for any period of time, and only a loving mother and wife can understand just how unbearable it is. You worry endlessly that your family is going to be ok. You feel helpless, as whatever happens while you are in your dungeon is completely out of your control. To miss out on once in a lifetime things, like graduations and birthdays is heartbreaking. There were many days that I did not know how I was going to get through it. Many days that I laid in my bunk and just cried and cried with no hope.

Yet I did get through it. The strength came from some unknown source. And then when I finally did get home, I had hoped that things would be as if I had never left. That was not the case, however. I lost a job that I loved, was appreciated for, and was really good at. A job that now is gone forever as they took away my radiology license and I cannot get it renewed. I have lost many family and friends, people that I would have never thought would turn their backs on me. Whenever I do leave home now, I don't want to see anyone that I know for fear of embarrassment. Most people only know what they read in the news about me. To date, the truth has never been told.

And to top it off - when I did get home I had to undergo two shoulder surgeries for an injury I sustained while incarcerated. An injury that was unattended to while I was in prison. I am undergoing physical therapy on a regular basis and may need a third surgery. Because of this injury I have not been able to return to the workplace in any capacity.

I hope and pray every day that I can get my life back, that I can pick up the pieces and have a normal life with my family again. It's almost beyond hope that somehow, I can make up for the lost two years when I was cruelly separated from my husband and children.

# CHAPTER NOTES

Chapter 1
New Yorker Magazine, Crossing Christie by Ryan Lizza dated April 14, 2014
The High Price I Had to Pay by Jamila Davis
NJ Spotlight, Bridget Ann Kelly Breaks Long Silence on Bridgegate, Calls
    Wildstein a "Liar" by Meir Rinde dated April 2, 2015

Chapter 8
Ruthless Ambition, the Rise and Fall of Chris Christie by Louis M. Manzo
The Jersey Sting by Ted Sherman and Josh Margolin

Chapter 12
Asbury Park Press, Little Egg Harbor Democrats get Death Threats by Eric
    Larsen dated November 8, 2015
Barnegat Manahawkin Patch, Waretown Man Shot and Killed by Police,
    Pointed Gun at Officers says Prosecutor by Graelyne Brashear dated Feb-
    ruary 9, 2012
Asbury Park Press, NJ Cop Charged in Dog Attack on Driver by Margaret F.
    Bonafide dated April 11, 2014
Asbury Park Press, Tape Spurs Use-of-Force Review by Matt Pais dated Janu-
    ary 8, 2009

CHAPTER 1 – PICTURE 1-2

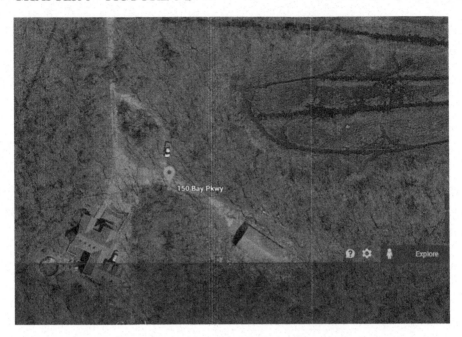

## CHAPTER 2 – DOCUMENT 1

**Direct - R. Parise - Ryan**

```
1        A.      Yes, Van Pelt was on the north

2    side, he was on the south side.  Actually, he sat

3    on the land use board.

4        Q.      Did he disqualify himself from the

5    application?

6        A.      No, actually he did not.

7    Actually, at the land use board meeting, and we

8    have the tapes of the meetings and the opinions,

9    he got up as a neighbor and protested against the

10   subdivision and how they should hit us with the

11   highest assessments possible.

12       Q.      Were you at that meeting?

13       A.      I was not.   My wife was.

14       Q.      Because I reviewed minutes of the

15   meeting where he got up, identified himself as

16   Gordan Von Schmidt and the board attorney told

17   him since he was a member of the board, that he

18   should not speak and that he should have his wife

19   speak, and he essentially sat down.

20       A.      I don't know what you were given,

21   but I have the minutes from the township with

22   their transcripts and that is not so.

23       Q.      All right.   The recorded

24   conversation with Mr. Mackie, is that one that's

25   been transcribed or is that only on audio?
```

**JOSEPH ALBANESE & ASSOCIATES**

Chapter 2 - Document Ia

Steven E. Yost, Esq. - it would be proper except for the fact that we have this deed restriction which runs with the land, which is pre-existing, which was part of a resolution previously approved which calls for no subdivision in the area until Walker Lane is paved. That was what was agreed to by the owner of the property at the time, there is a restriction on the deed and it runs with the land. I can understand why an applicant wouldn't want to pave any further distance than they would have to but the problem is that you have that restriction on the deed.

Chairman Avellino - I believe that this isn't the first time that people have come before the Board to subdivide the property on Walker Lane. This is one of the reasons this ended up on the deed restriction.

Steven E. Yost, Esq. - so unless there is some evidence that this is paved, according to the standards of our Engineer, I don't think we can hear this application.

Dennis Tredy - I agree

Steven E. Yost, Esq. - that is my legal opinion

Dennis Tredy - if that is the legal interpretation and we hired you as our Lawyer, I think that is what we have to do.

Vincent Anepete - in order to take his advice, the Chair has to deny hearing the application.

Brian Lonergan - I don't think you can even carry it because you can't hear it until the road is paved.

Barbara Wolford - they would also have to re-notice

Tara Musselman - they would have to go before the Township Committee to see if the Town is open to improving Walker Lane and they would have to be willing to improve the entire Walker Lane.

Chairman Avellino - exactly

Tara Musselman - if the Township Committee wanted, would you pave the entire Walker Lane?

Marjorie Parise -I don't even know where Walker Lane ends.

Anthony Mercuro - its about 1800' long from Elizabeth to the end and there is no defined end. That is still something that is undefined.

William Somerville - it is defined on the tax map.

Tara Musselman - they would have to get a survey to see exactly where it ends.

Dennis Tredy - we are being helpful to those individuals. I am not calling them applicants because I don't believe it is a legitimate application.

Chairman Avellino - I would like to Board to vote on whether we should hear this application. Tara Musselman made a motion to follow legal advice and not hear the application, seconded by Brian Lonergan. Roll Call: Ayes - Musselman, Lonergan, Kraft, Mercuro, Tredy, Anepete, Avellino Motion carried.

*William Somerville resumed his seat on the Board*

**PUBLIC COMMENT**

Chairman Avellino - can I have a motion to open the meeting to public comment? Tara Musselman made a motion to open to the public, seconded by Brian Lonergan. Ayes - All the public is welcome to come forward to open a discussion to anything.

Gordon VonSchmidt - 21 Walker Lane came forward. My personal feeling on Walker Lane, probably the best way I could put it when I commented before was, if we are talking about an improvement to a particular area, maximum building to me means maximum improvement. In this particular case, the applicant wants to take this parcel of land and push it to the maximum. I think it warrants maximum improvements, I think it warrants an entire paved road, I think it warrants curbs and sidewalks. If an individual wants to stick with bear minimums and build a house or whatever, then I

## CHAPTER 2 – DOCUMENT 3

## CHAPTER 2 – DOCUMENT 3a

RESOLUTION

**04-44**

WHEREAS, the Ocean Township Municipal Utilities Authority of Ocean County, New Jersey, has been duly formed according to N.J.S.A 40:14B-1 et seq.; and

WHEREAS, there exists a need for the Extension of Water on Walker Lane for the proper maintenance and operation of the OCEAN TOWNSHIP MUNICIPAL UTILITIES AUTHORITY and there are funds available for same;

NOW THEREFORE, BE IT RESOLVED BY THE OCEAN TOWNSHIP MUNICIPAL UTILITIES AUTHORITY OF THE TOWNSHIP OF OCEAN, COUNTY OF OCEAN AND STATE OF NEW JERSEY, as follows:

1. The award of contract for the Extension and Installation of Water Main on Walker Lane, be awarded to Total Building Services, 1467 West Bay Avenue, Barnegat, New Jersey, 08005 in the amount of ten thousand eight hundred fifty dollars ($10,850.00).

CERTIFICATION

I, Jack B. Layton, Jr., Secretary of the Ocean Township Municipal Utilities Authority, do hereby certify that the foregoing Resolution was duly passed at the Regular Meeting of the Authority held on June 16, 2004.

Jack B. Layton, Jr.

Secretary

## CHAPTER 2 – DOCUMENT 2a

*Chapter 2 - Document 2a*

# Richard A. Alaimo Associates

200 High Street, Mt. Holly, New Jersey 08060 Tel: 609-267-8310 Fax: 609-267-7452
2 Market Street, Paterson, New Jersey 07501 Tel: 973-523-6200 Fax: 973-523-1765

August 3, 2009

Ms. Marlene Miller
Township of Ocean
50 Railroad Avenue
Waretown, NJ 08758-8818

Re: Township of Ocean
K&R Custom Builders
Panse Minor Subdivision
Pavement Escrow Allocation
Our File: M-311-173

Dear Ms. Miller:

Pursuant to your recent request, we have prepared the following statement with respect to the escrow allocation for the paving of Walker Lane. I have been informed by the County that the cost of the paving of Walker Lane was $26,748. This work consisted of an overlay pavement 1,915 LF in length and 24 feet wide (45,960 SF).

Proportioning a half-width of 12 feet for the 463 LF of the approved lots comes to the amount of $3,233.50 for the County roadway improvement across the frontage of these approved lots.

Should you have any questions concerning this matter, please call.

Very truly yours,

RICHARD A. ALAIMO ASSOCIATES

Martin G. Miller, PE, PLS, PP, CME
Senior Project Engineer

MGM:lhr
cc: Marge Panse, K&R Custom Homes, LLC (146 Mary Bell Road, Barnegat, NJ 08005)
Kenneth J. Monca, Township Administrator, Township of Ocean
Diane B. Ambrosio, Township Clerk, Ocean Township

## - Consulting Engineers -

Civil • Structural • Mechanical • Electrical • Environmental • Planners

## CHAPTER 2 – DOCUMENT 2

Receipt of the above check is acknowledged on this __24th__ day of November, 2003

_Marleen J. Miller_
Signature
Print name: _Marleen J. Mi_
Print Title: _Treasurer_

Witness:

_Marjorie Parise_
Marjorie PARISE

_Robert Parise_
ROBERT PARISE

Parise (Way) - 8232

## CHAPTER 2 – DOCUMENT 4

20; Hooper Avenue, Toms River, NJ   08753-7807
TEL: 732-473-3400   FAX: 732-473-3408

**T&M ASSOCIATES**

# Fax

To: Howard Botwinsky     From: Ton Margolis

Fax:   609.296 7287     Pages: 82

Phone:   296 3103     Date: 11/20/03

Re.     CC:

☐ Urgent   ☐ For Review   ☐ Please Comment   ☐ Please Reply   ☐ Please Recycle

● Comments:

Howard,

This was sent for Joe Coronato.

## CHAPTER 2 – DOCUMENT 5

Q. If you didn't know whether or not there was a deadline for filing in the tax court,
how do you know whether the municipality perceived that they were in this box?

A. Okay. I used the word check mate.

Q. That's it. I'm sorry. Thank you. How do you know whether or not the
municipality considered them in check mate?

A. Well, the municipality and Joe
Coronado, their solicitor, were concerned about their overall conduct in the way they treated the
whole application, and they were also concerned with Joseph Gannon, who apparently was some kind of
friend or colleague. Joseph Gannon was Mr. and Mrs. Parise's first attorney And Mr. Coronado expressed to me in
the meeting that we had with him that overall, his goal was consistent with our goal, which was not to file the litigation,
is not what Bob wanted, but to help him get approval for the project. So they denied the default approval, and Coronado sent a letter saying
don't give him a default approval, and yet, when it was determined that they were taxing the property
as if they had gotten the approval, they were somewhat over a barrel. That's what I'm talking about in check mate, ignoring the fact in the tax
appeal. What we were trying to accomplish and what we did accomplish was Mr. Coronado's statement to
me is this can all work out, Bob can bring his application in, he is going to probably get some kind of project.
Coronado doesn't have to worry about the board getting sued, which we had already
threatened to do, Mr. Gannon doesn't have to worry about getting sued for malpractice because if Bob
and Marge get a development, everybody is happy. That's the leverage of the check mate that I was
talking about.

Q. Okay. When did this conversation occur? When was the first time this subject matter - when did it occur?

A. Before and during these meetings -- the meeting that we had with Mr. Coronado and his engineer and our engineer and Mr. Parise and I.

Q. Can you give me a month and a year?

A. Maybe November 2003. I know there's memos and billings and information that can confirm all of that.

CHAPTER 3 – PICTURE 1

# CHAPTER 5 – DOCUMENT 1

**Shore Community Bank**
SHORE COMMUNITY BANK
1012 HOOPER AVENUE
TOMS RIVER, NEW JERSEY 08753

*** *BUSINESS LOAN ANNUAL NOTICE* ***

*AS OF 12/31/14*

| | |
|---|---|
| LOAN NUMBER | 000155900188 |
| LOAN BALANCE | .00 |
| INTEREST RATE | 6.000 |
| ESCROW BALANCE | .00 |
| TAX ID NUMBER | 02-0721815 |

0767-00256

PARIS LAND, LLC
146 MARY BELL RD
MANAHAWKIN NJ 08050-7826

PRINCIPAL PAID BY YOU THIS YEAR................ 70,194.15
INTEREST APPLICABLE FOR THIS TAX YEAR.......... .00

---

**Shore Community Bank**
SHORE COMMUNITY BANK
1012 HOOPER AVENUE
TOMS RIVER, NEW JERSEY 08753

*** *BUSINESS LOAN ANNUAL NOTICE* ***

*AS OF 12/31/14*

| | |
|---|---|
| LOAN NUMBER | 000155200323 |
| LOAN BALANCE | 50,337.71 |
| INTEREST RATE | 8.250 |
| ESCROW BALANCE | .00 |
| TAX ID NUMBER | 02-0721815 |

0767-00197

PARIS LAND, LLC
146 MARY BELL RD
MANAHAWKIN NJ 08050-7826

PRINCIPAL PAID BY YOU THIS YEAR................ 12,505.00
INTEREST APPLICABLE FOR THIS TAX YEAR.......... .00

Shore
Community
Bank

SHORE COMMUNITY BANK
1012 HOOPER AVENUE
TOMS RIVER, NEW JERSEY 08753

*** BUSINESS LOAN ANNUAL NOTICE ***

AS OF 12/31/14

| LOAN NUMBER | 000156200178 |
|---|---|
| LOAN BALANCE | .00 |
| INTEREST RATE | 4.250 |
| ESCROW BALANCE | .00 |
| TAX ID NUMBER | 02-0721815 |

0767-00312

PARIS LAND, LLC
146 MARY BELL RD
MANAHAWKIN NJ 08050-7826

PRINCIPAL PAID BY YOU THIS YEAR................ 37,733.00
INTEREST APPLICABLE FOR THIS TAX YEAR.......... .00

---

Shore
Community
Bank

SHORE COMMUNITY BANK
1012 HOOPER AVENUE
TOMS RIVER, NEW JERSEY 08753

*** BUSINESS LOAN ANNUAL NOTICE ***

AS OF 12/31/14

| LOAN NUMBER | 000156200130 |
|---|---|
| LOAN BALANCE | .00 |
| INTEREST RATE | 4.250 |
| ESCROW BALANCE | .00 |
| TAX ID NUMBER | 02-0721815 |

0767-00306

PARIS LAND, LLC
146 MARY BELL RD
MANAHAWKIN NJ 08050-7826

PRINCIPAL PAID BY YOU THIS YEAR................ 35,361.00
INTEREST APPLICABLE FOR THIS TAX YEAR.......... .00

Shore
Community
Bank

SHORE COMMUNITY BANK
1012 HOOPER AVENUE
TOMS RIVER, NEW JERSEY 08753

ᴬᴬᴬ **BUSINESS LOAN ANNUAL NOTICE** ᴬᴬᴬ

AS OF 12/31/14

| | |
|---|---|
| LOAN NUMBER | 000155100102 |
| LOAN BALANCE | .00 |
| INTEREST RATE | 8.500 |
| ESCROW BALANCE | .00 |
| TAX ID NUMBER | 02 0721815 |

PARIS LAND, LLC
146 MARY BELL RD
MANAHAWKIN NJ 08050-7826

PRINCIPAL PAID BY YOU THIS YEAR............... 250,000.00
INTEREST APPLICABLE FOR THIS TAX YEAR.......... .00

CHAPTER 6 – DOCUMENT 1

**From:** Joseph Bondy <josephbondy@mac.com>
**Date:** May 30, 2009 12:29:28 PM EDT
**To:** Robert Parise <KRCUSTOMHOMES@COMCAST.NET>
**Subject: Re:**

Things sound promising. I got a call from Matt Skahill, from the USAO in Newark, returning my call and asking for the tapes!

McKenna knows the case, let's meet Friedman, and maybe your team has just gelled.

Caught some Largemouth Bass, Catfish and Perch in Central Park this a.m. w/ my son...

Moss. Moss. Moss.

## CHAPTER 7 – DOCUMENT 1

U.S. Department of Justice

*United States Attorney*
*District of New Jersey*

970 Broad Street, Suite 700         (973) 645-2700
Newark, NJ 07102         fax (973) 645-2857

February 20, 2009

**By Hand Delivery To:**
Joseph Bondy, Esq.

          R·BERT
      Re: ~~Joseph Parise~~    + MARJORIE PARISE

Dear Mr. Bondy:

             ROBERT + MARJORIE PARISE
     With respect to the interview of ~~Joseph Parisi~~ by representatives of the United States Attorney's Office for the District of New Jersey, and the FBI to be held today ("the interview"), the following terms and conditions apply.

     1. Should your client be prosecuted, no statements made by your client during the interview will be used against your client in the government's case-in-chief at trial or for purposes of sentencing, except as provided below.

     2. The government may use any statement made or information provided by your client, or on your client's behalf, in a prosecution for false statements, perjury, or obstruction of justice, premised on statements or actions during or subsequent to the interview.

     3. The government may make derivative use of and may pursue any investigative leads suggested by any statements made or other information provided by your client and may use the evidence or information obtained therefrom against your client in any manner.

     4. The government may use your client's statements and any information provided by your client to cross-examine your client and to rebut any evidence or arguments offered on your client's behalf.

     5. Neither this letter nor the interview constitutes a plea discussion. In the event this letter or the interview is later construed to constitute a plea discussion, your client knowingly and voluntarily waives any right your client might have under Fed. R. Evid. 410, Fed. R. Crim. P. 11(f), or otherwise, to prohibit the use against your client of statements made or information provided during the interview.

     6. Neither this letter nor the interview requires the government to enter into any plea discussions with your client or to file any motion regarding cooperation provided by your client. Furthermore, neither this letter nor the interview constitutes the timely provision of

complete information to the government concerning your client's involvement in an offense, within the meaning of Section 3E1.1(b)(1) of the Sentencing Guidelines.

      7. No statements made by your client during the interview shall be used directly to determine the applicable Sentencing Guidelines range, except as set forth in the final sentence of this paragraph. However, the government may use such statements and any other information provided by your client to pursue investigative leads suggested thereby and may use any evidence or information generated by its investigation directly against your client to determine the applicable guideline range. Moreover, with regard to sentencing, the government may use the statements made and the information provided by your client during the interview to cross-examine your client and to rebut any evidence or arguments offered on your client's behalf. In addition, the government may disclose to the Probation Office and the Court any statements made and information provided by your client and may use such statements and information to determine where within a given guideline range your client should be sentenced and to oppose any downward departure or downward adjustment.

      Very truly yours,

      RALPH J. MARRA, JR.
      Acting United States Attorney

      By: Adam S. Lurie
      Assistant U.S. Attorney

- 2 -

153

# CHAPTER 9 – DOCUMENT 1

CERTIFIED PUBLIC ACCOUNTANTS AND CONSULTANTS

TWO FOREST AVENUE, ORADELL, NEW JERSEY 07649

201-599-0008 • FAX: 201-599-0095 • WWW.GCS-CPA.COM

March 5, 2007

Robert and Marjorie Parise
146 Mary Bell Road
Barnegat, New Jersey 08005

**PERSONAL & CONFIDENTIAL**

**ENGAGEMENT LETTER FOR PROFESSIONAL SERVICES**

Dear Robert and Marjorie:

Based upon our discussions, we are pleased to present the following engagement letter for professional services to be rendered to Paris Custom Homes, Inc., K&R Custom Homes, Inc. and the related individuals, Robert and Marjorie Parise, including Paris Land, LLC. If you have any questions regarding any element of this letter, please do not hesitate to contact me.

**SERVICES TO BE PROVIDED**

We will provide the following professional services for the years 2003, 2004, 2005 and 2006:

1. *General Accounting Assistance:* We will be available on an "as needed" basis to provide assistance to you with respect to recording transactions, making journal entries, financial reporting issues and any other accounting information system or accounting questions that may arise during the course of the year.

2. *Management Meetings:* We will be available on an "as needed" basis to participate in management/planning meetings regarding financial matters, organizational matters, financial planning, estate planning, operations, etc., at the request of the principals.

3. *Corporate Tax Planning:* You will provide us with an estimate of 2007 income for Paris Custom Homes, Inc. and K&R Custom Homes, Inc. Based upon these estimates, we will advise you regarding year-end bonus amounts and applicable withholding requirements.

4. *Tax Compliance-Corporations:* We will prepare the Federal and New Jersey State corporation income tax returns for the years ended December 31, 2003, 2004, 2005 and 2006 for Paris Custom Homes, Inc. and K&R Custom Homes, Inc.

Robert and Marjorie Parise
March 5, 2007
Page 2.

## SERVICES TO BE PROVIDED (CONT.)

5. *Payroll Tax Compliance*: We will prepare the 2007 Federal and New Jersey State payroll tax returns and the annual 1099 and 1098 forms for Paris Custom Homes, Inc., K&R Custom Homes, Inc. and Paris Land, LLC.

6. *Tax Compliance and Planning-Individuals:* We will provide tax compliance services for the following individuals for 2003, 2004, 2005 and 2006:

    * Robert and Marjorie Parise (Including Paris Land, LLC)

7. *General Advisory Services:* We will be available on an "as needed" basis to provide the following general business advisory services:

    * Advanced tax planning
    * Financial planning
    * Estate planning
    * Banking, credit facilities
    * Mergers, acquisitions, sale of business
    * Organizational consulting
    * Succession planning, management transitions
    * Performance improvement
    * Retirement plans
    * Compensation plans
    * Asset acquisitions, divestitures
    * Entity selection, planning, inter-company transactions
    * General business advisory services

## INVESTMENT IN OUR SERVICES

Based upon our experience with other similar engagements, your investment in our services will be as follows:

| Service | Fee |
| --- | --- |
| 1. General Accounting Assistance | Hourly as required |
| 2. Management Meetings | Hourly as required |
| 3. Tax Planning | Projection / Bonus Calculations - $750<br>Advanced Planning – Hourly as required |
| 4. Tax Compliance-Corporations | $16,000 - $18,000 (for both companies) |
| 5. Payroll Tax Compliance | $1,000 - $1,500 (for both companies) |
| 6. Tax Compliance-Individuals | $6,000 - $7,000<br>Planning – Hourly as Required |
| 7. General Advisory Services | Hourly as Required |

155

Robert and Marjorie Parise
March 5, 2007
Page 3.

## INVESTMENT IN OUR SERVICES (CONT.)

Our hourly rates currently range between $145 and $295 depending on the nature of the work being done and the level of the professional performing the services. Out-of-pocket expenses will be billed separately. Every effort will be made to keep our professional time to a minimum, consistent with the requirements of the engagement. Any fee quoted above as "hourly as required" will be discussed with you before the work is performed when possible. Certain "special projects" need to be done on an emergent basis that may preclude a detailed determination of the project fees.

Invoices for our services will be rendered as our work progresses and are payable upon presentation.

Our engagement is not designed to detect fraud or defalcations that may exist. However, we will inform you of any such circumstances that may come to our attention unless these items are clearly inconsequential.

Department of Treasury Circular 230 requires that we notify you that under the terms of this engagement (i) no written statement to be provided by us relating to any Federal tax transaction or matter is intended to be used, and no such statement can be used by the taxpayer, for the purpose of avoiding penalties that may be imposed on the taxpayer and (ii) such written statement may not be used by any person to support the promotion or marketing of or to recommend any Federal tax transactions or matters.

If this letter correctly sets forth your understanding of the terms of our engagement, kindly sign a copy of this letter in the space provided below and return a copy to us.

We are pleased to submit this engagement letter and we appreciate the opportunity you have presented to us. If you have any questions regarding this letter, please contact me. We look forward to the opportunity to serve you.

In order to begin our engagement, we will require a retainer in the amount of $5,000.

Sincerely,

**GRAMKOW, CARNEVALE, SEIFERT & CO., LLC**

Ted A. Carnevale, CPA
Chief Executive Officer

Agreed and accepted:

_____          _____
Robert Parise                                                Date

_____          3-22-07
Marjorie Parise                                              Date

# CHAPTER 9 – DOCUMENT 2

**U.S. Department of Justice**
United States Attorney's Office
District of New Jersey
Peter Rodino Federal Bldg.
970 Broad St., Suite 700
Newark, NJ 07102
Phone: (973) 645-2893
Fax: (973) 297-2069

July 29, 2008

Marjorie Parisi
146 Mary Bell Rd
Barnegate, NJ 08005

Re: United States v. BRIAN WINTERS
    Case Number 2005R00311 and Court Docket Number: 08-246

Dear Marjorie Parisi:

The United States Department of Justice believes it is important to keep victims of federal crime informed of court proceedings. This notice provides information about the above-referenced criminal case.

Defendant BRIAN WINTERS has been sentenced by the Court. The Court ordered the defendant to the following:

Incarceration of 46 month(s)
Followed by Supervised Release of 3 year(s)
The Court further ordered the following special condition(s): Drug or Alcohol Treatment

The Court ordered restitution to be paid in case 2005R00311 in the total amount of $215,750.00 to Marjorie Parisi. While the Court has ordered restitution in this case, it does not mean the defendant(s) will make restitution payments. In the event restitution payments are received from the defendant, the funds will be distributed by the Clerk of the United States District Court. It is your responsibility to keep our Office and the Clerk's Office advised of any address changes.

The Victim Notification System (VNS) is designed to provide you with information regarding the case as it proceeds through the criminal justice system. You may obtain current information about this case on the VNS web site at WWW.Notify.USDOJ.GOV or from the VNS Call Center at 1-866-DOJ-4YOU (1-866-365-4968) (TDD/TTY: 1-866-228-4619) (International: 1-502-213-2767). In addition, you may use the Call Center or Internet to update your contact information and/or change your decision about participation in the notification program. If you update your contact information to include a current email address, VNS will send information to that email address. In order to continue to receive notifications, it is your responsibility to keep your contact information current.

You will use your Victim Identification Number (VIN) '**1080324**' and Personal Identification Number (PIN) '**4696**' anytime you contact the Call Center and the first time you log on to the VNS web site. In addition, the first time you access the VNS Internet site, you will be prompted to enter your last name (or business name) as currently contained in VNS. The name you should enter is Parisi.

Remember, VNS is an automated system and cannot answer questions. If you have other questions which involve this matter, please contact this office at the number listed above.

Sincerely,

*Shirley Estreicher*

Shirley Estreicher
Victim Witness Coordinator

## CHAPTER 10 – DOCUMENT 1

HELLRING LINDEMAN GOLDSTEIN & SIEGAL LLP
Attorneys for Plaintiff, Eric R. Perkins,
    Chapter 7 Trustee for Global Trading Investment, LLC
One Gateway Center
Newark, New Jersey 07102-5386
(973) 621-9020
John A. Adler, Esq.

UNITED STATES BANKRUPTCY COURT
FOR THE DISTRICT OF NEW JERSEY

```
------------------------------X
In the Matter of:              :      Case No. 08-22743 (RTL)

MARJORIE PARISE,               :      Hon. Raymond T. Lyons

         Debtor,               :      Chapter 7 Proceeding
------------------------------X
ERIC R. PERKINS, Chapter 7     :      Adv. Proceeding No. 08-2428
Trustee for Global Trading
Investment, LLC; Brian David   :
Winters; Wyndham Group and
Excalibur Trust,               :      STIPULATION OF SETTLEMENT
                                      and DISMISSAL
         Plaintiffs,           :

v.                             :

MARJORIE PARISE,               :

         Defendant.            :
------------------------------X
```

This matter having been resolved by and between the
attorneys for the parties, it is hereby STIPULATED AND AGREED as
follows:

    1.    The defendant, Marjorie Parise, will pay in full

any of the required payments, and after a grace period of ten
(10) days, the Trustee may sell the vehicles and upon the filing
of an Affidavit with the Court, on notice to defendant's counsel,
reciting the default and sale, obtain a non-dischargeable
judgment against the defendant in the amount of $200,000, less
any monies which the defendant has paid and which the Trustee may
obtain from the sale of the vehicles.

     5.   The parties will exchange general releases which
will release all claims against the other except claims arising
out of this Stipulation. The releases will be held in escrow by
the Trustee's counsel subject to payment of the settlement amount
referred to above. Upon payment in full of the settlement
amount, the Trustee's counsel will forward the Trustee's release
to Marjorie Parise's counsel.

     6.   The settlement is subject to approval of the U.S.
Bankruptcy Court in accordance with Federal Rule of Bankruptcy
Court 9019. In the event the settlement is not approved, any
monies paid by Marjorie Parise on account of the settlement will
be forthwith refunded by the Trustee. The Notice of Settlement
will not be filed by counsel for the Trustee until the Trustee
has received the $40,000 down payment referred to in paragraph
1(A) of this Stipulation.

2

7.    Upon the approval of the Settlement by the Court, the plaintiff will dismiss this action with prejudice and without costs subject to being reopened for the purpose of entering the judgment referred to in paragraph 4 above.

HELLRING LINDEMAN GOLDSTEIN & SIEGAL, LLP
Attorneys for Plaintiff, Eric A. Perkins, Trustee


By: _____
JOHN A. ADLER
A Member of the Firm

Dated: MAY    , 2009


By: _____
JULES L. ROSSY, ESQ.
Attorney for Defendant Marjorie Parise

_Marjorie Parise_
MARJORIE PARISE


Dated: May 28, 2009

160

CPSIA information can be obtained
at www.ICGtesting.com
Printed in the USA
BVOW06s1830011116
466621BV00014B/162/P